50 Magical Fairy Designs

An Adult Coloring Book

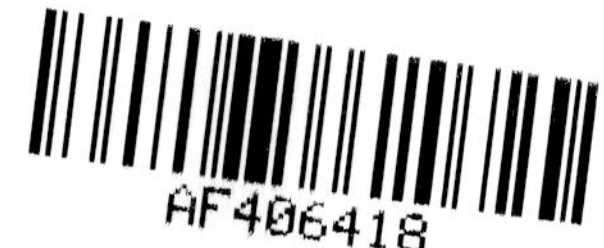

HUE COLORING

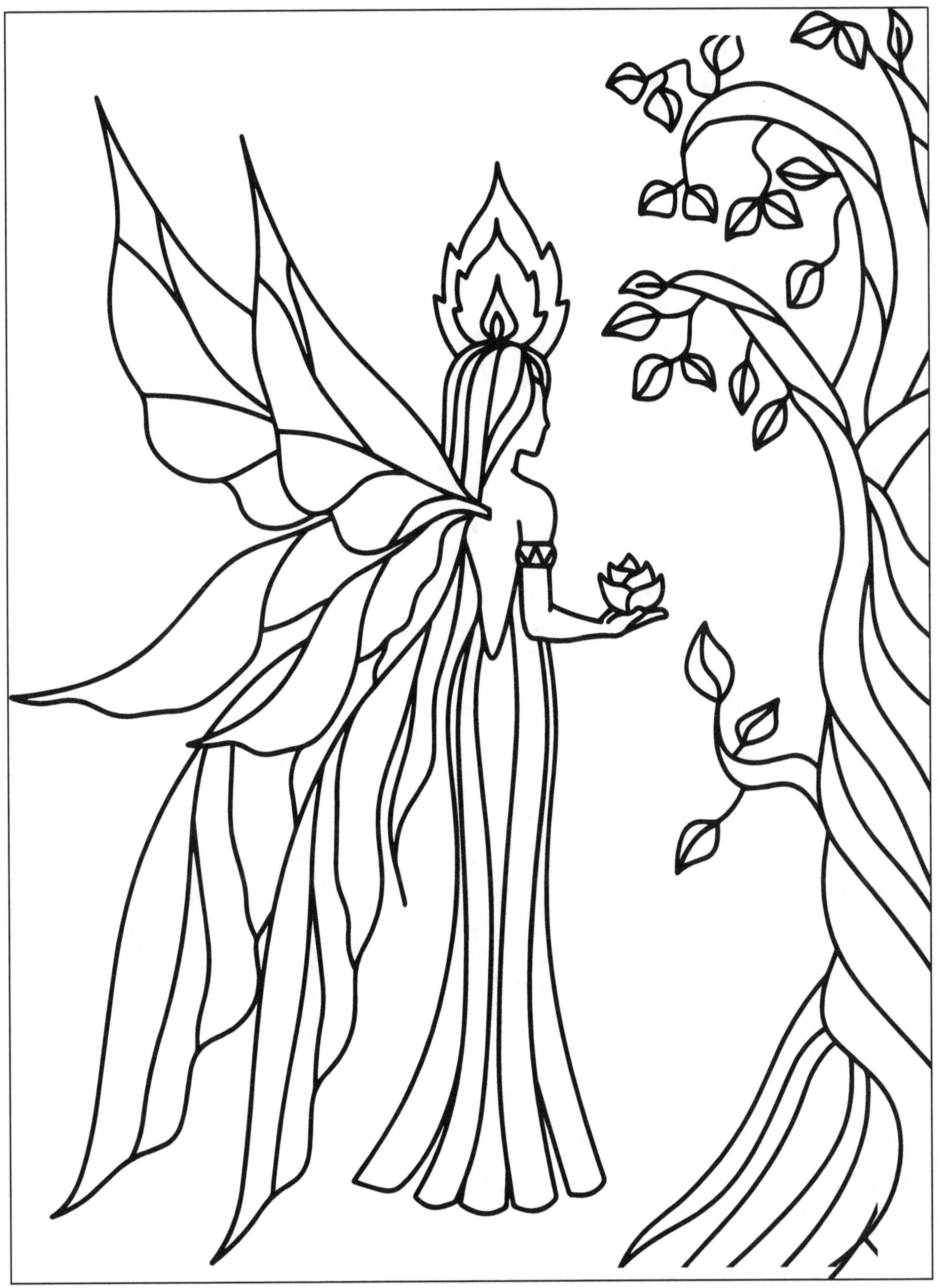

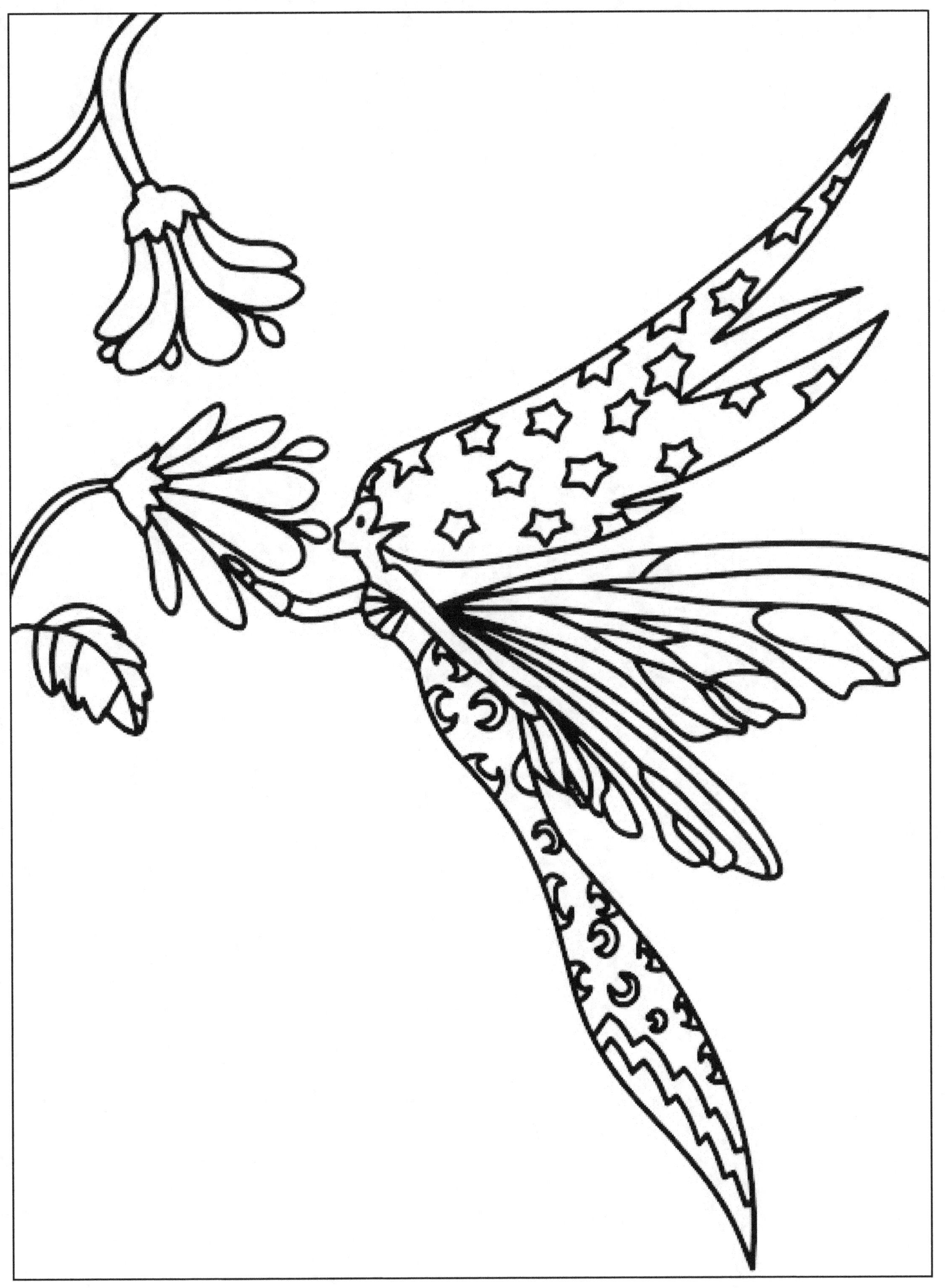

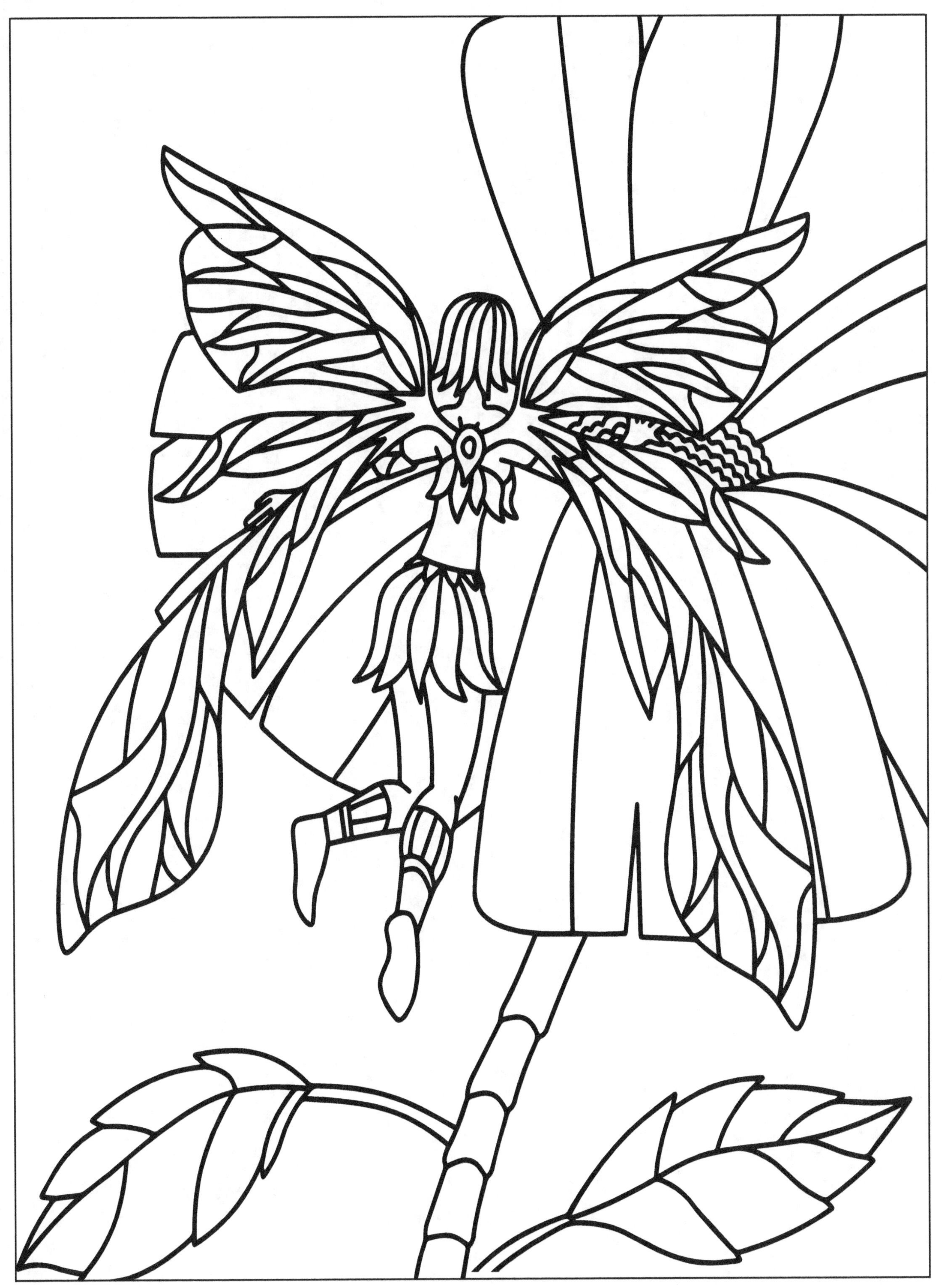

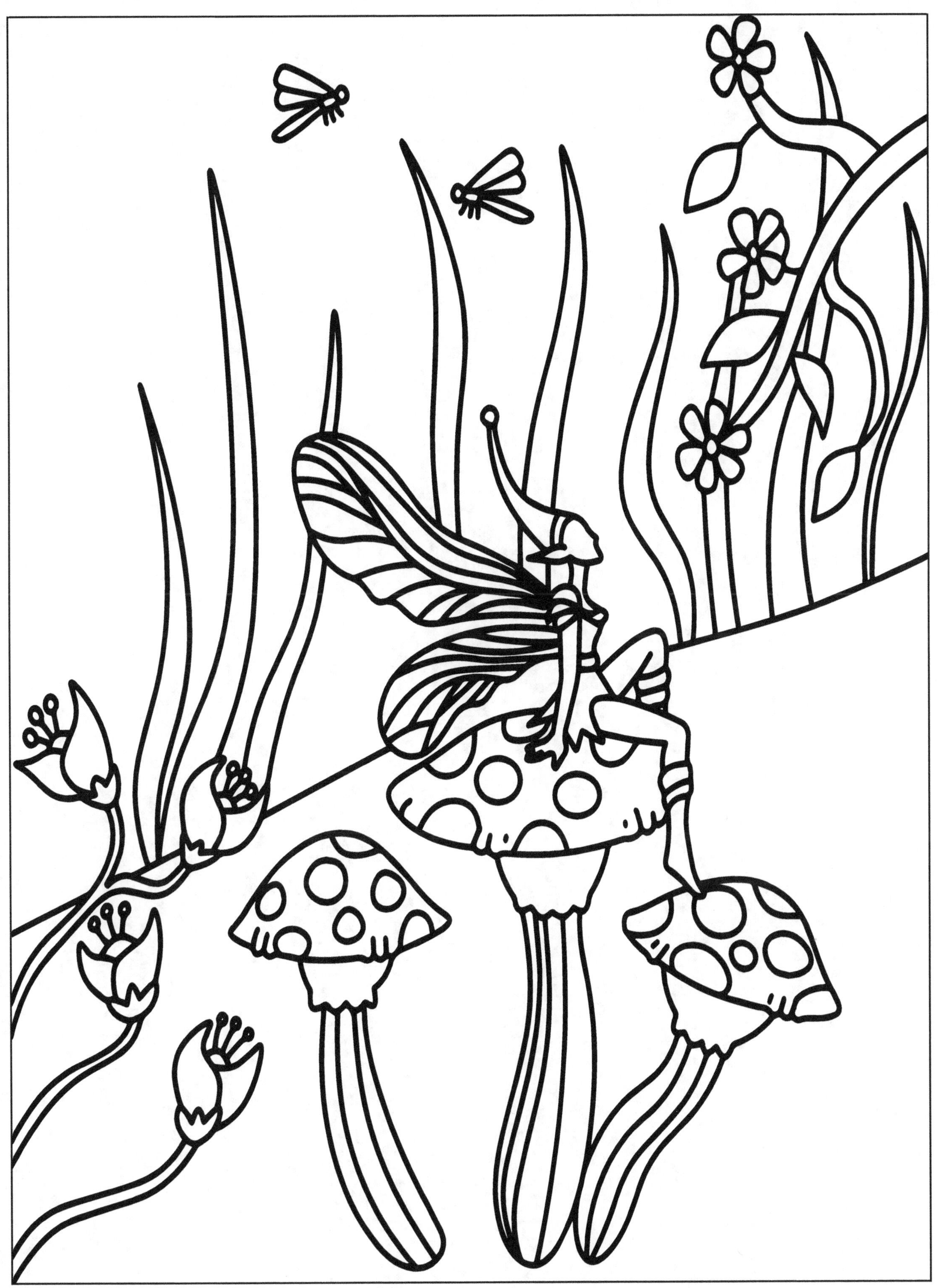

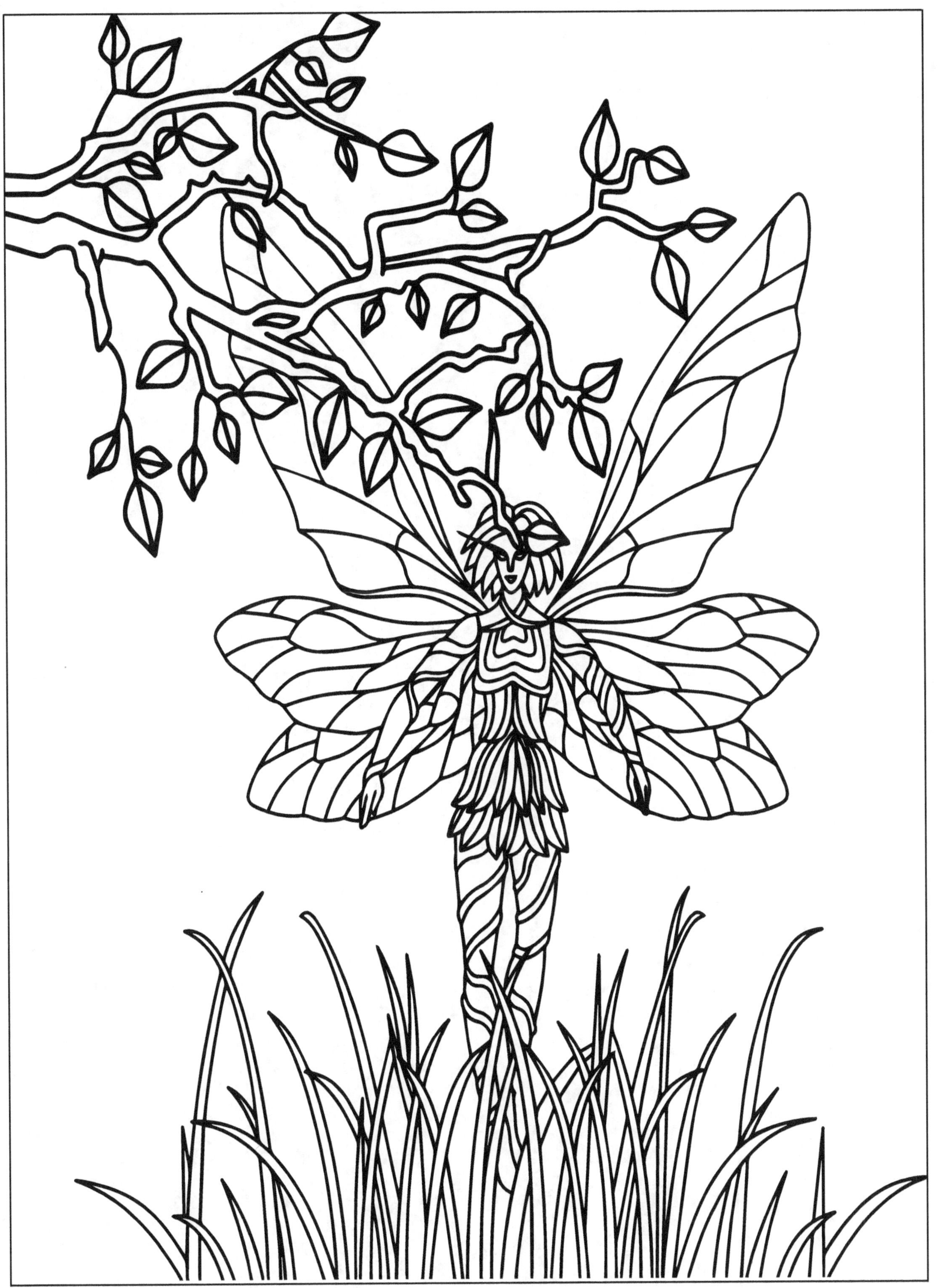

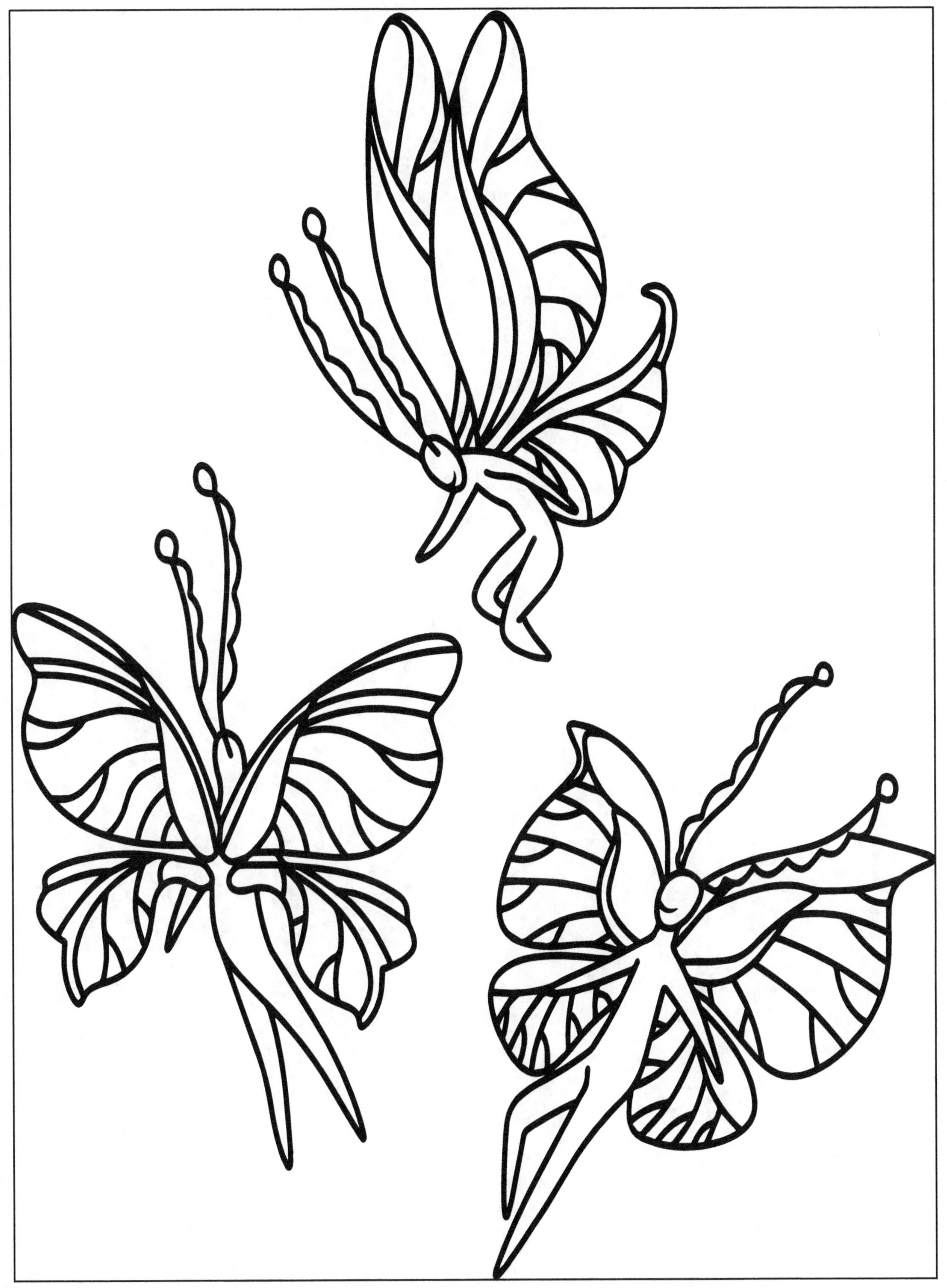

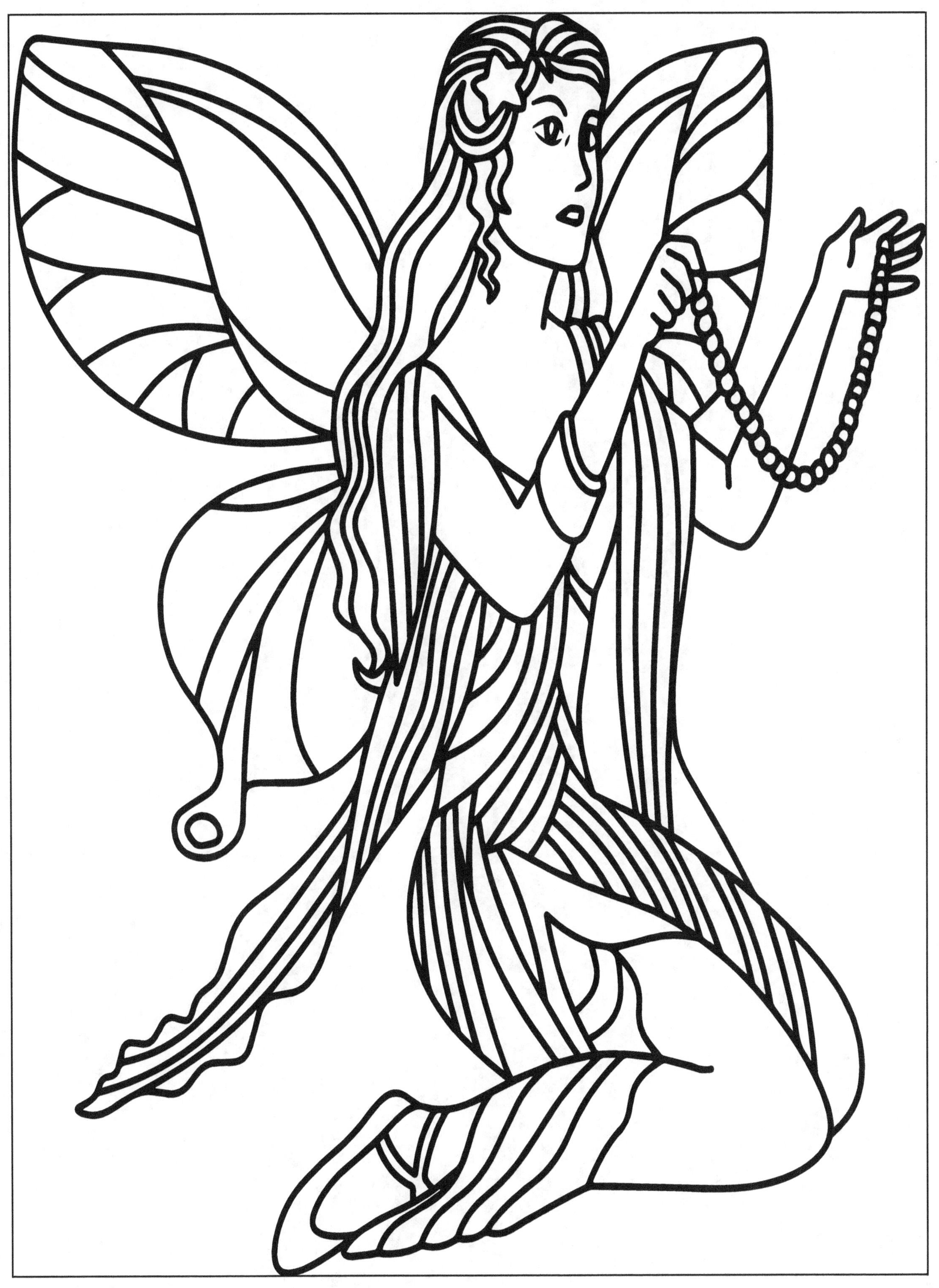

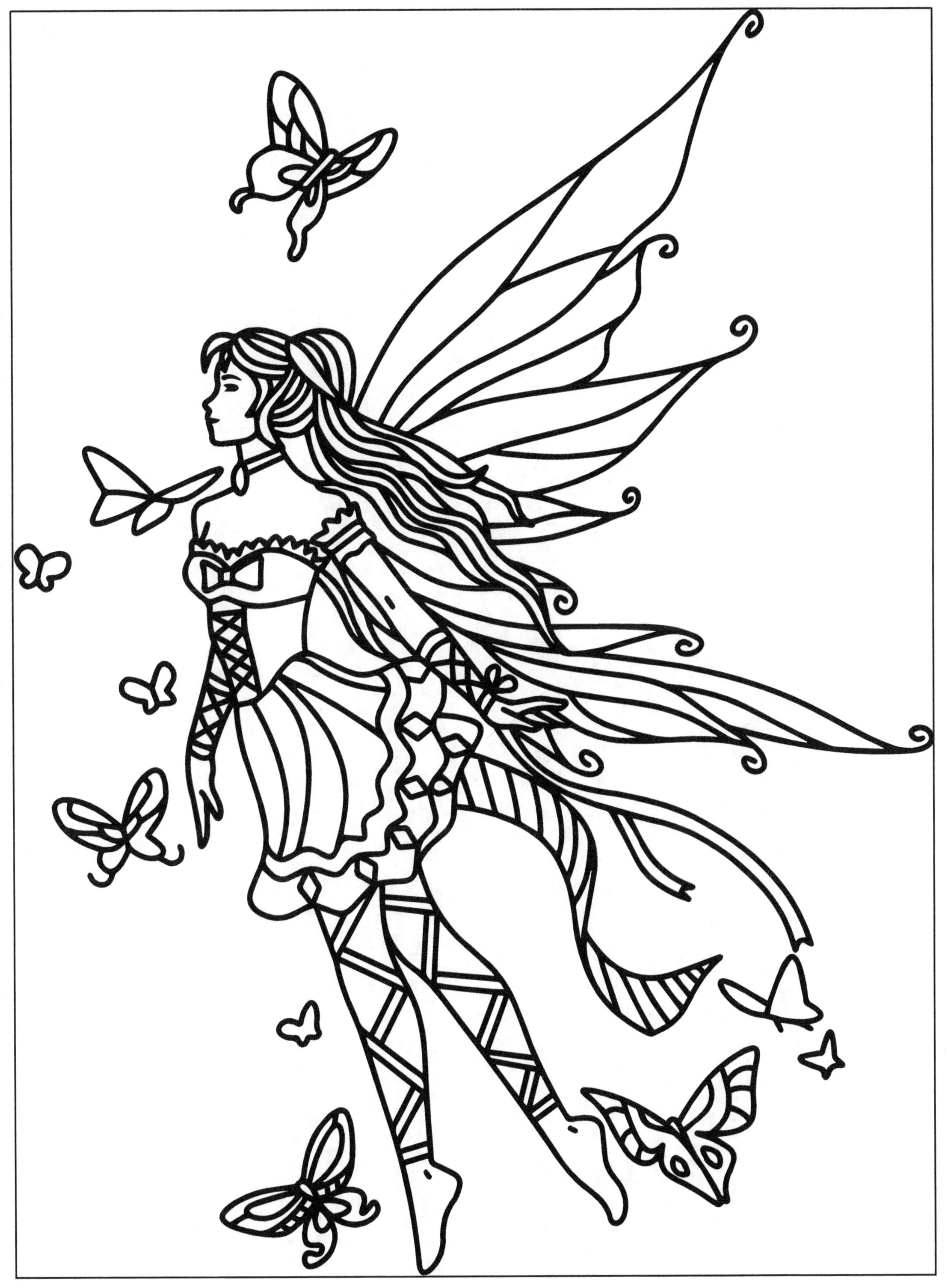

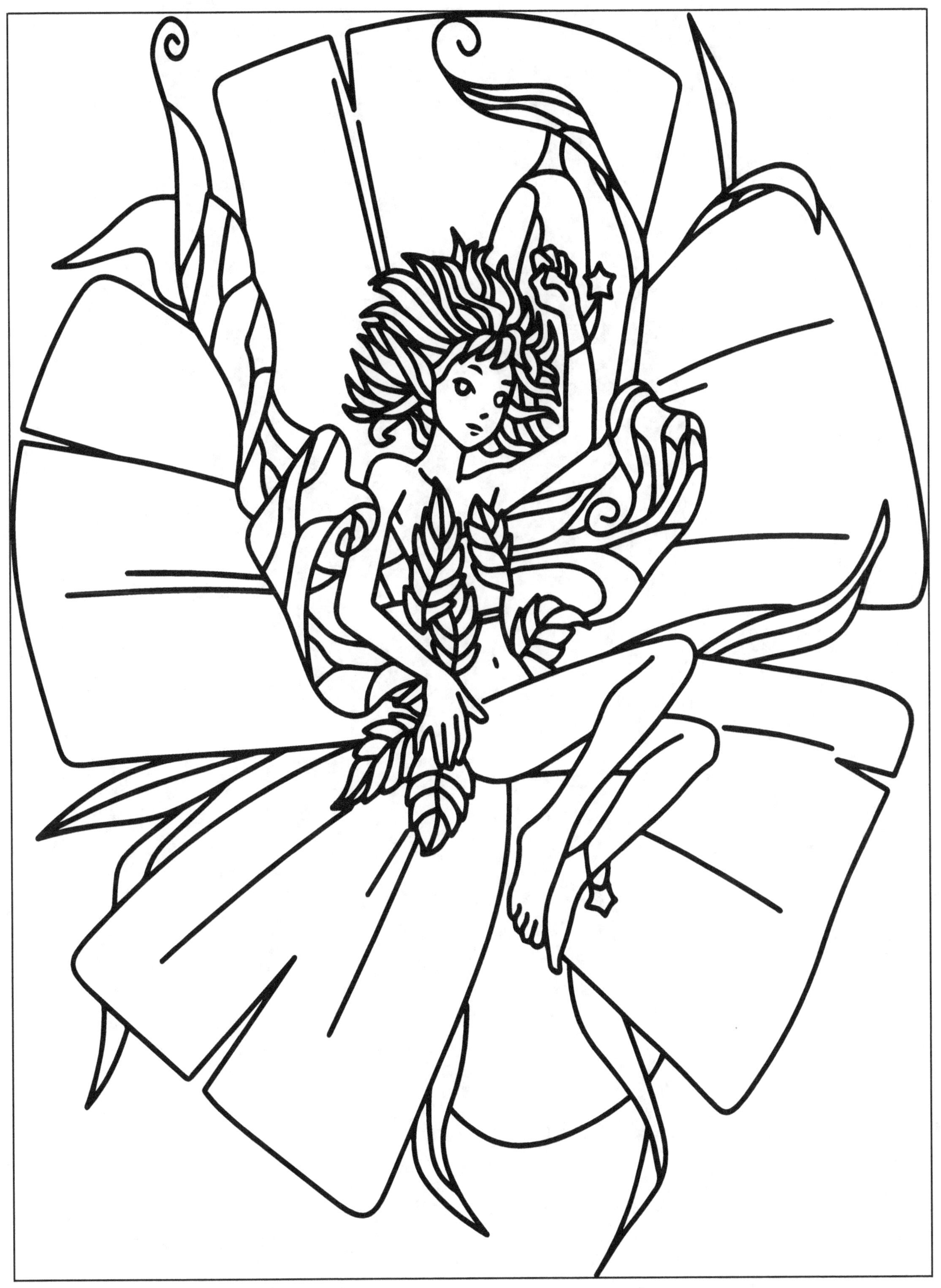

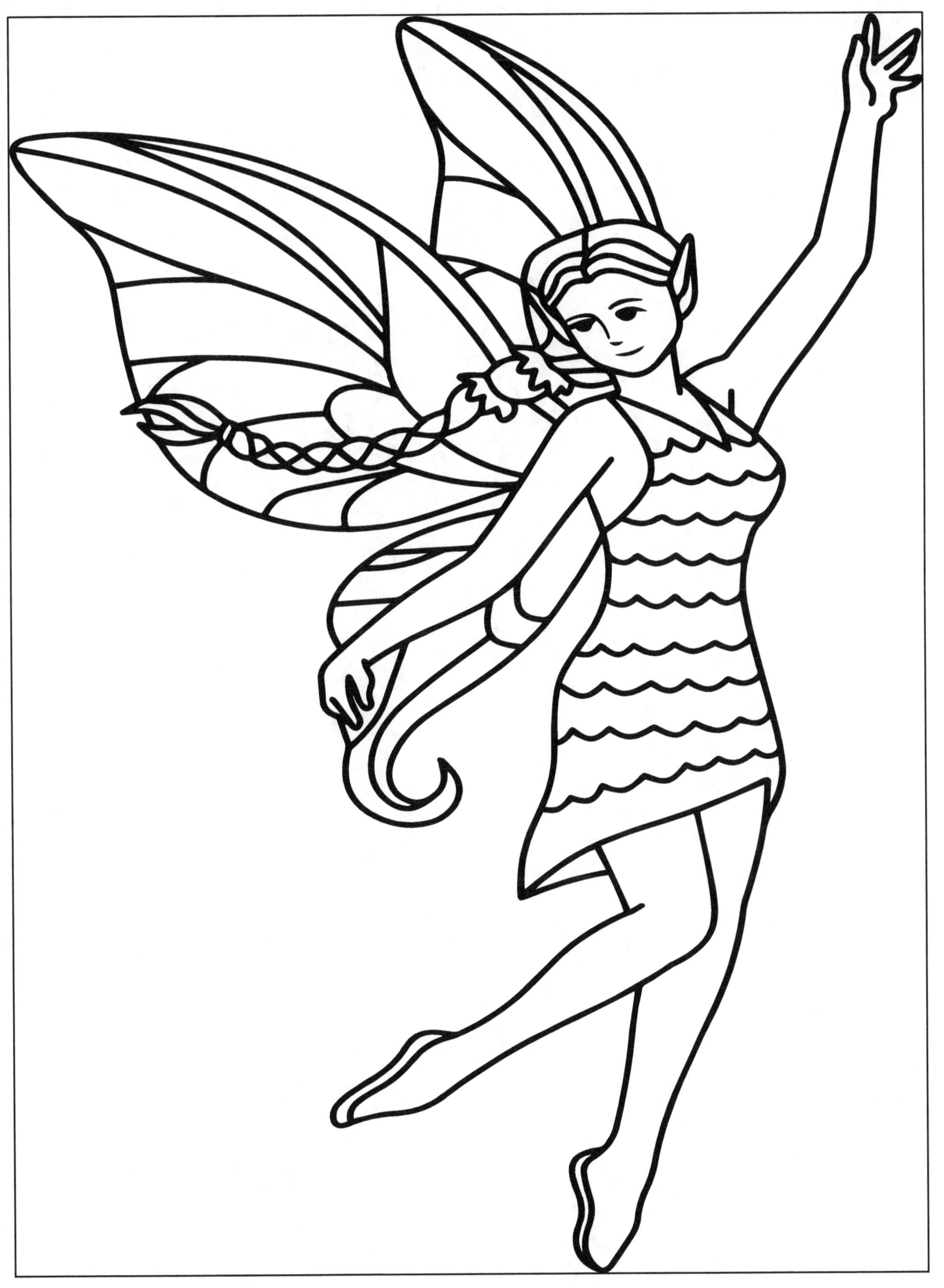

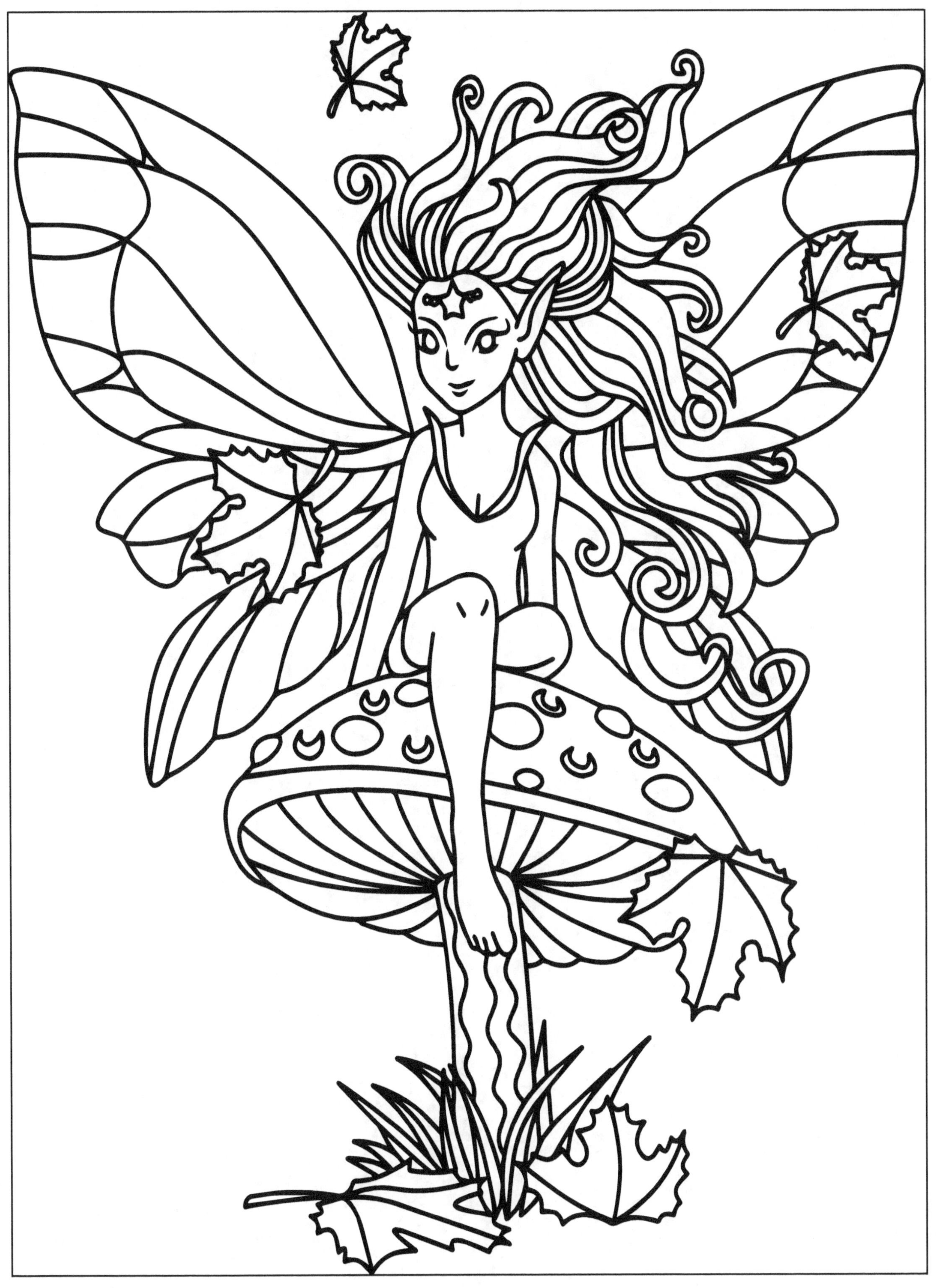

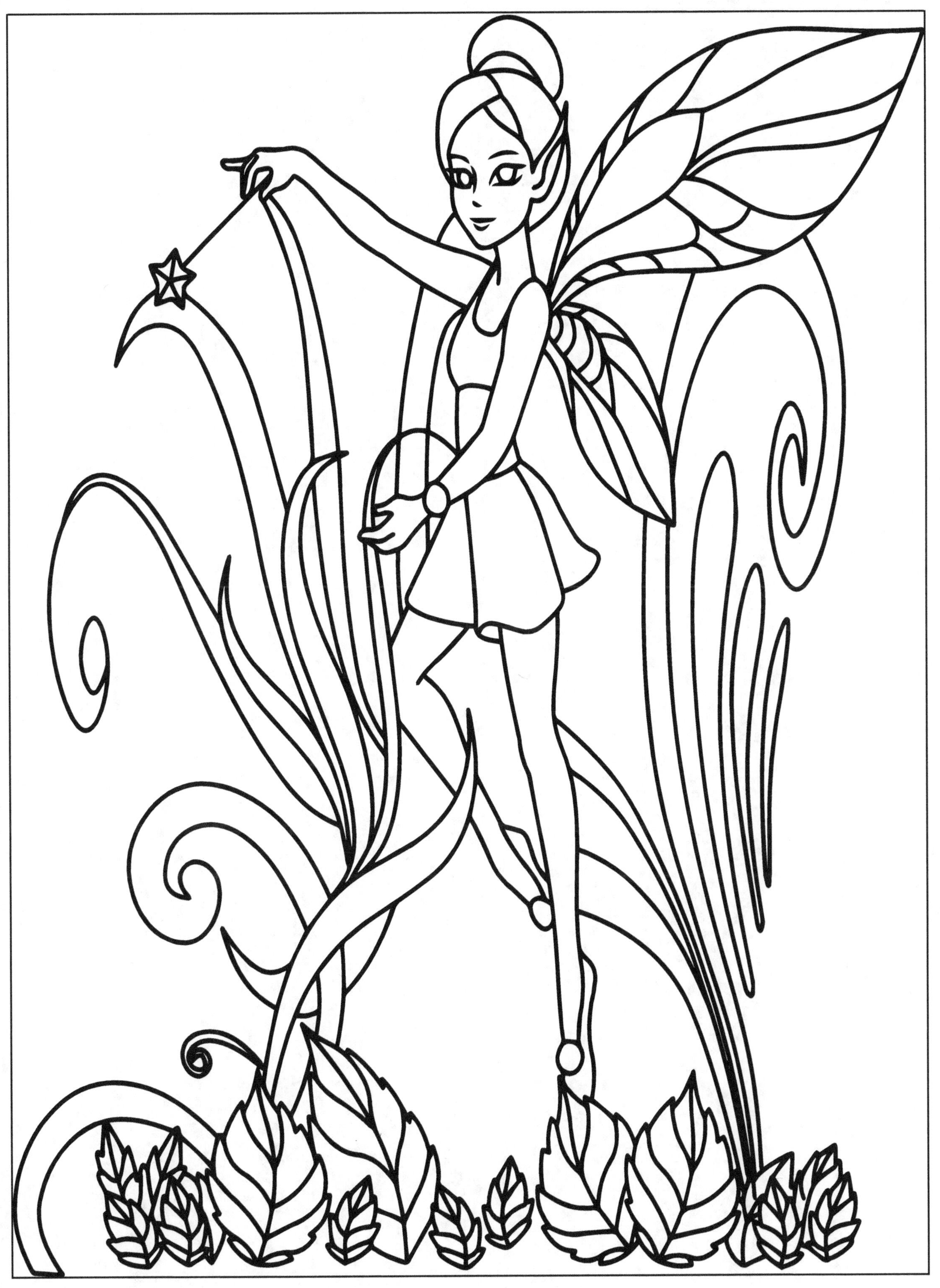

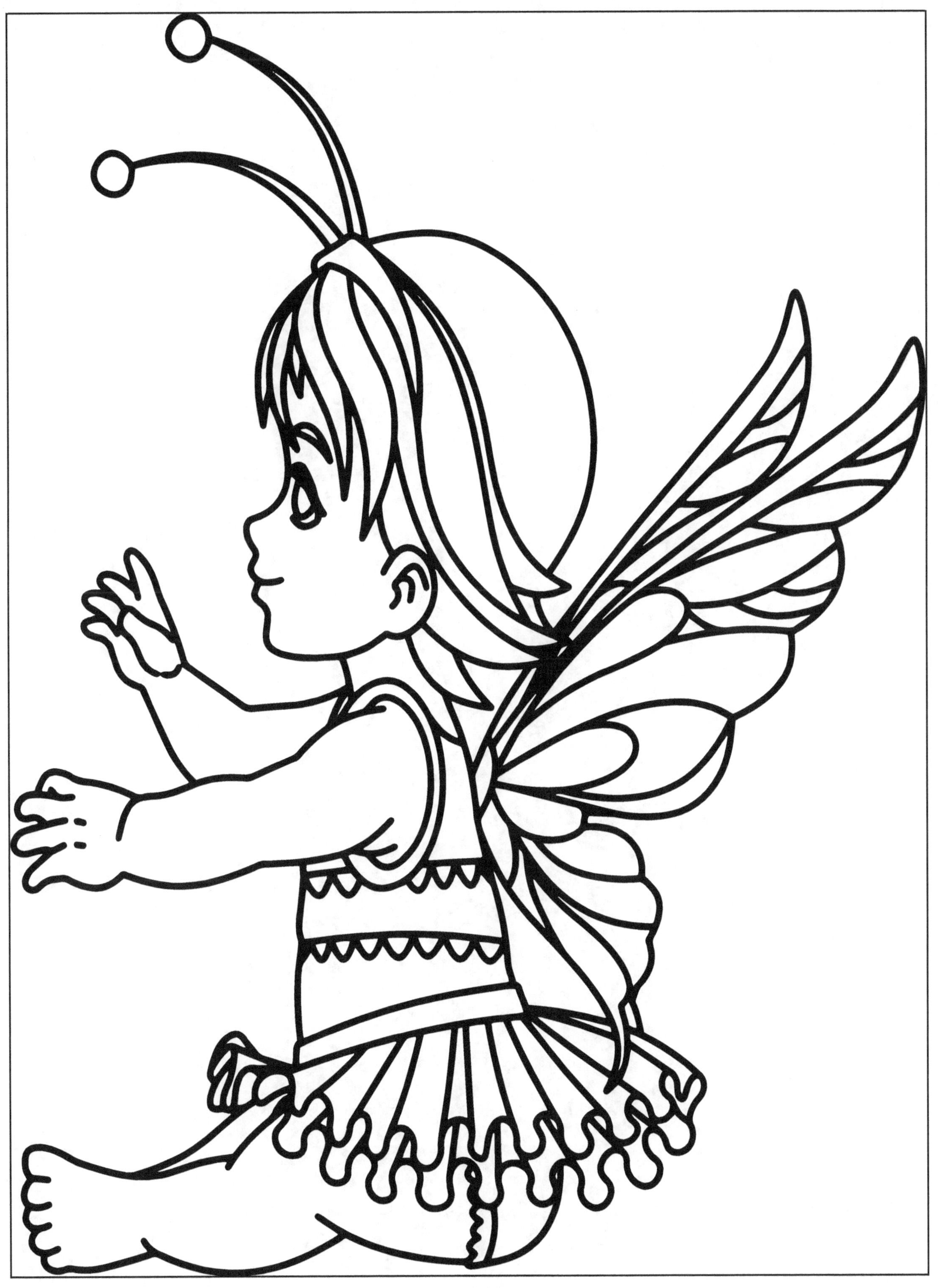

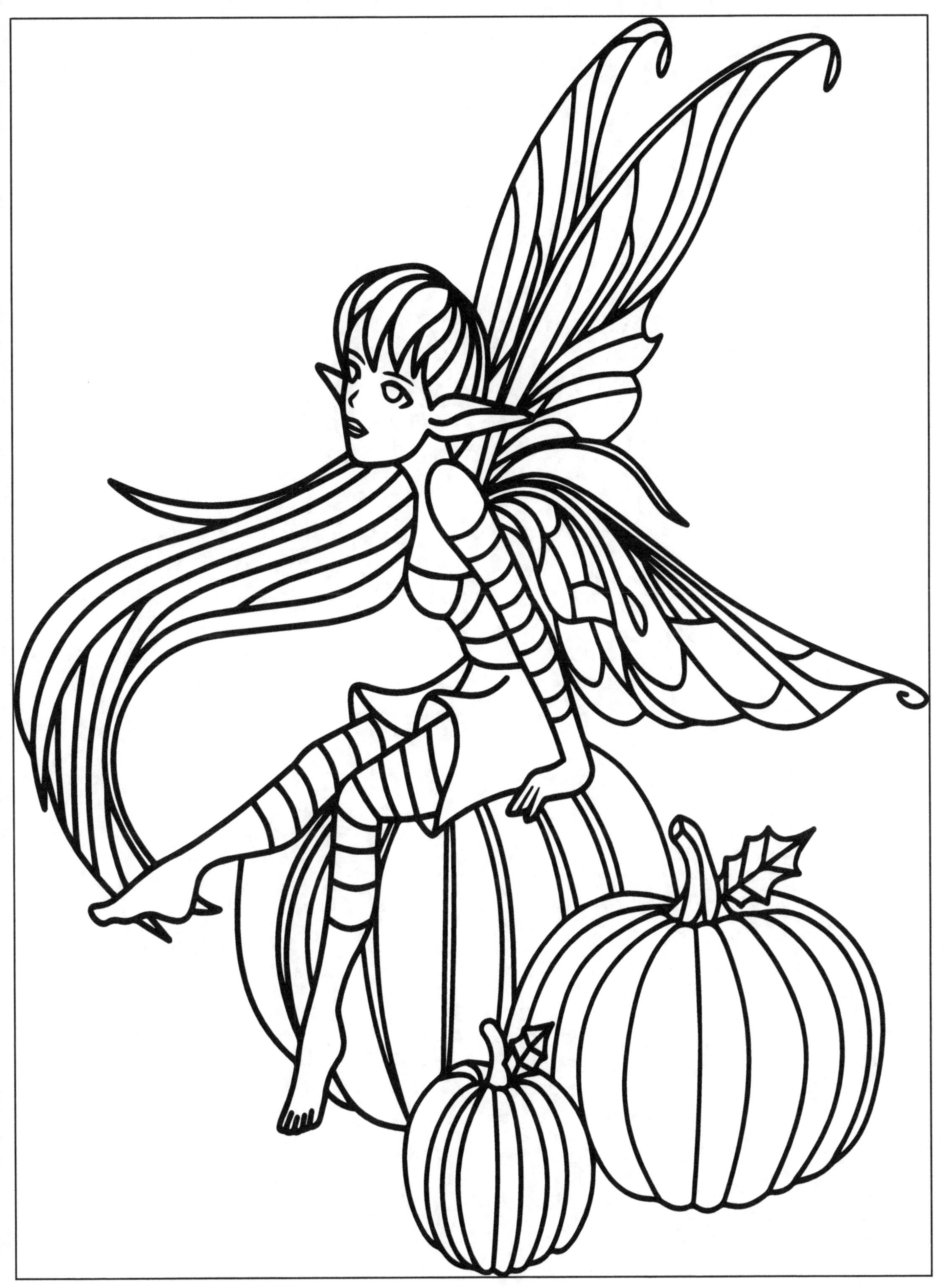

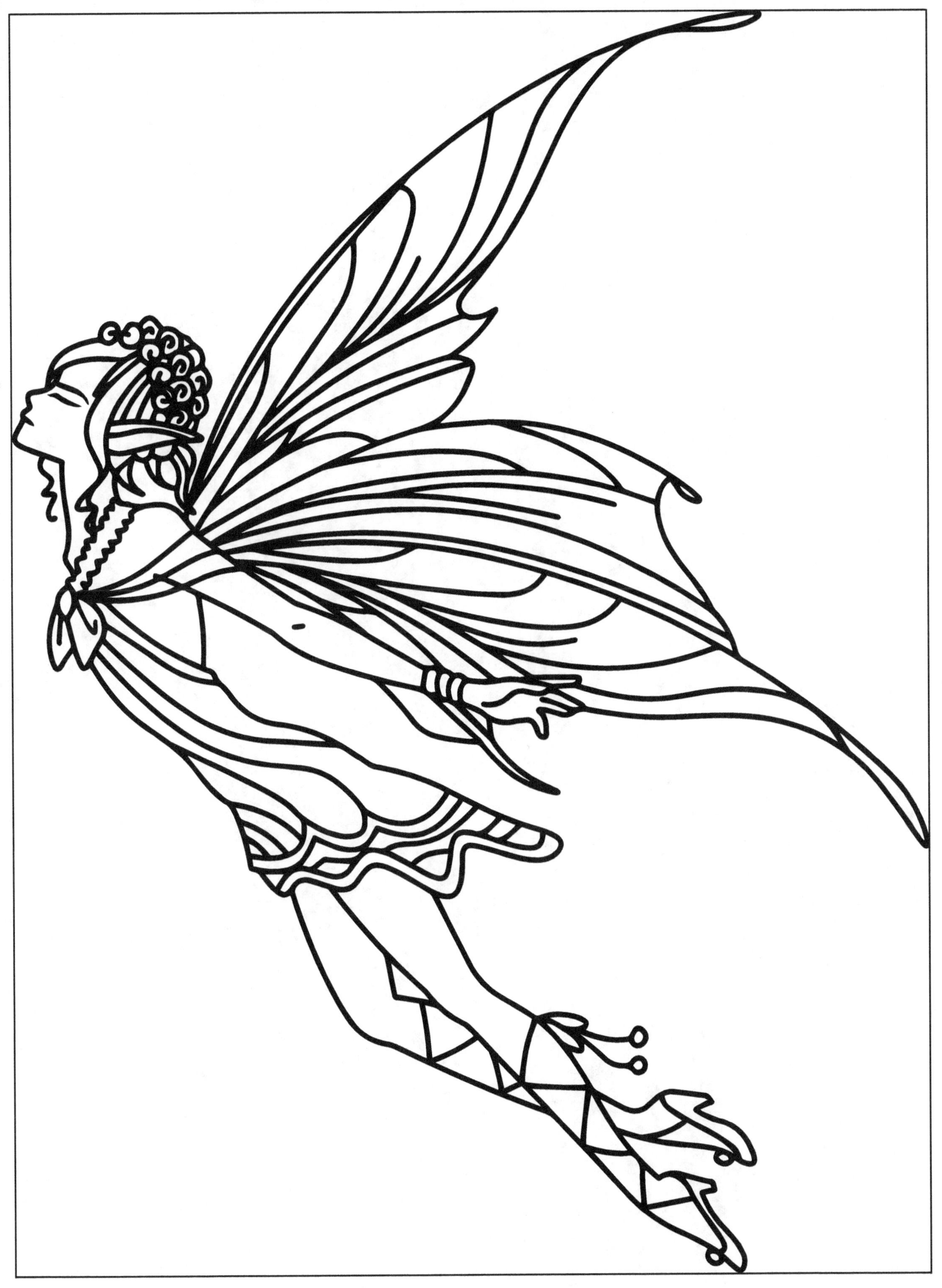

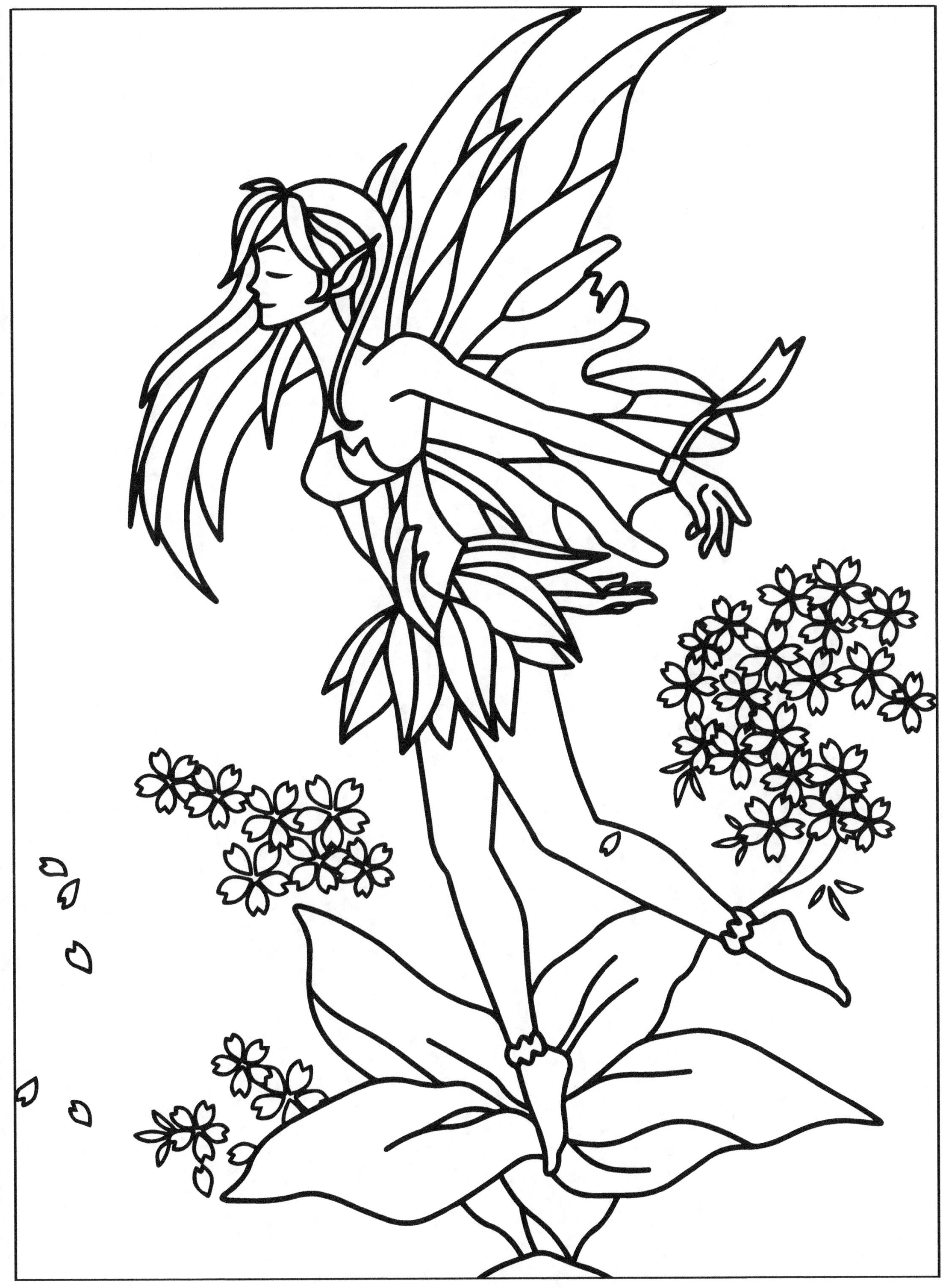

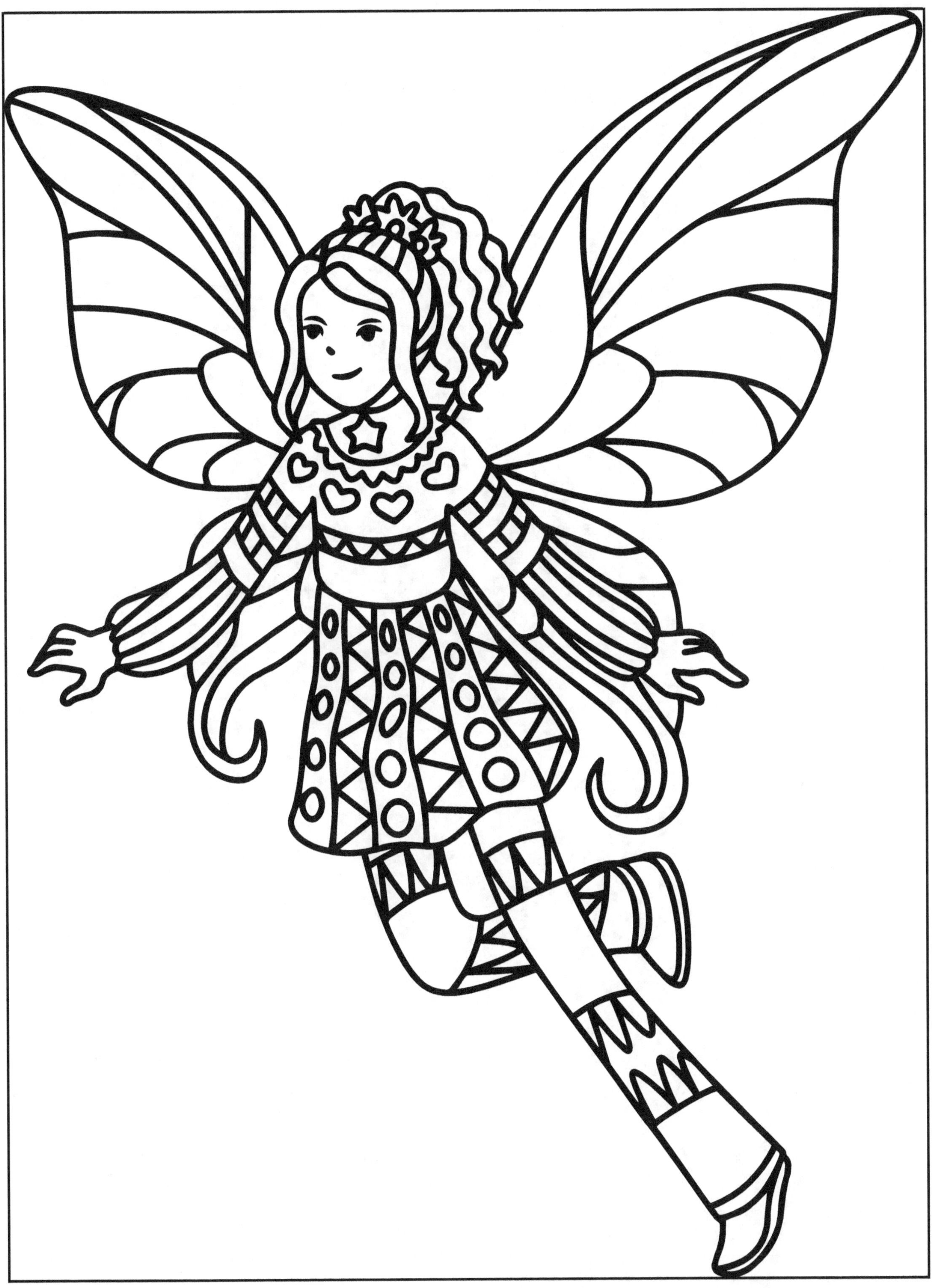

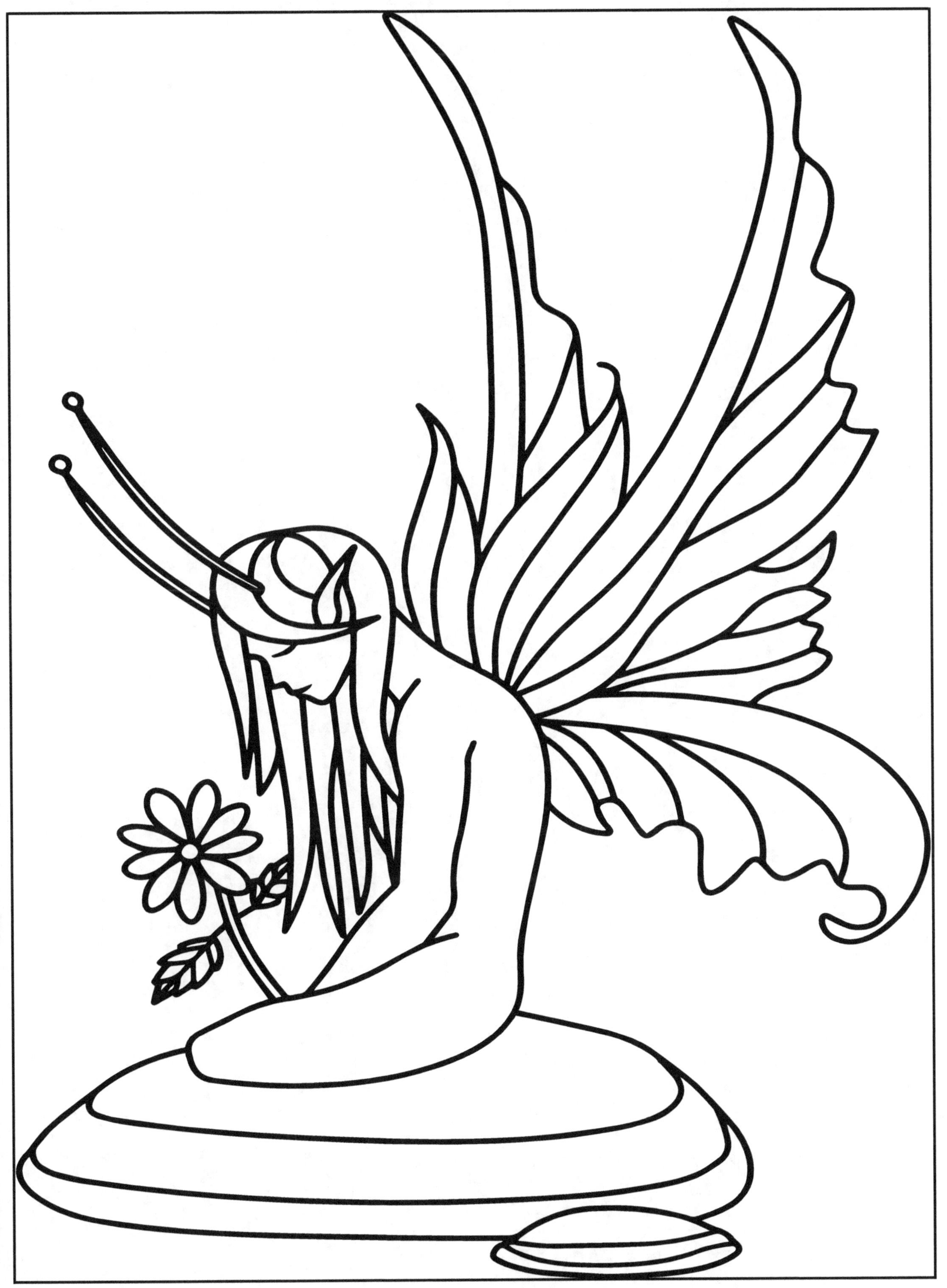

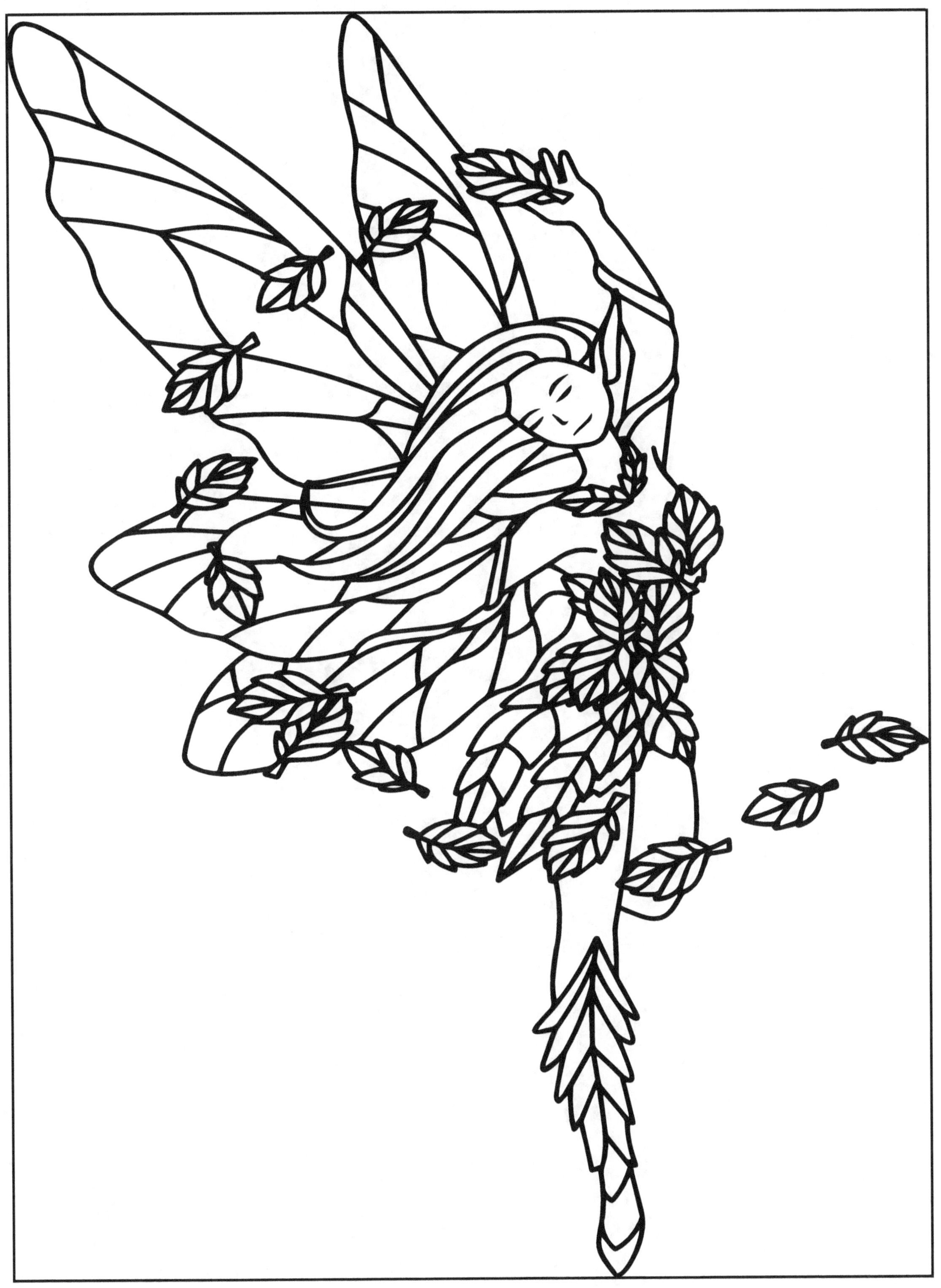

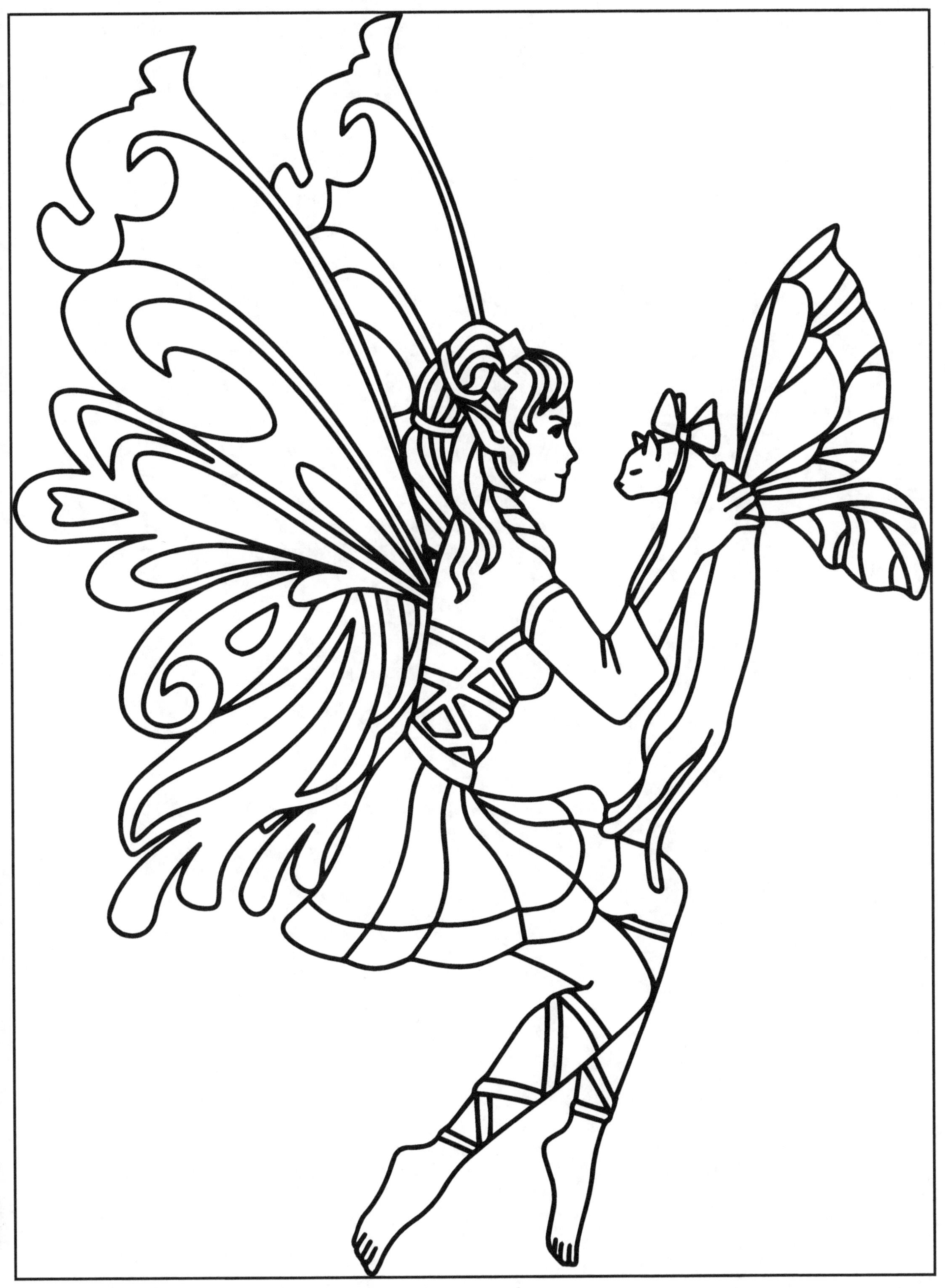

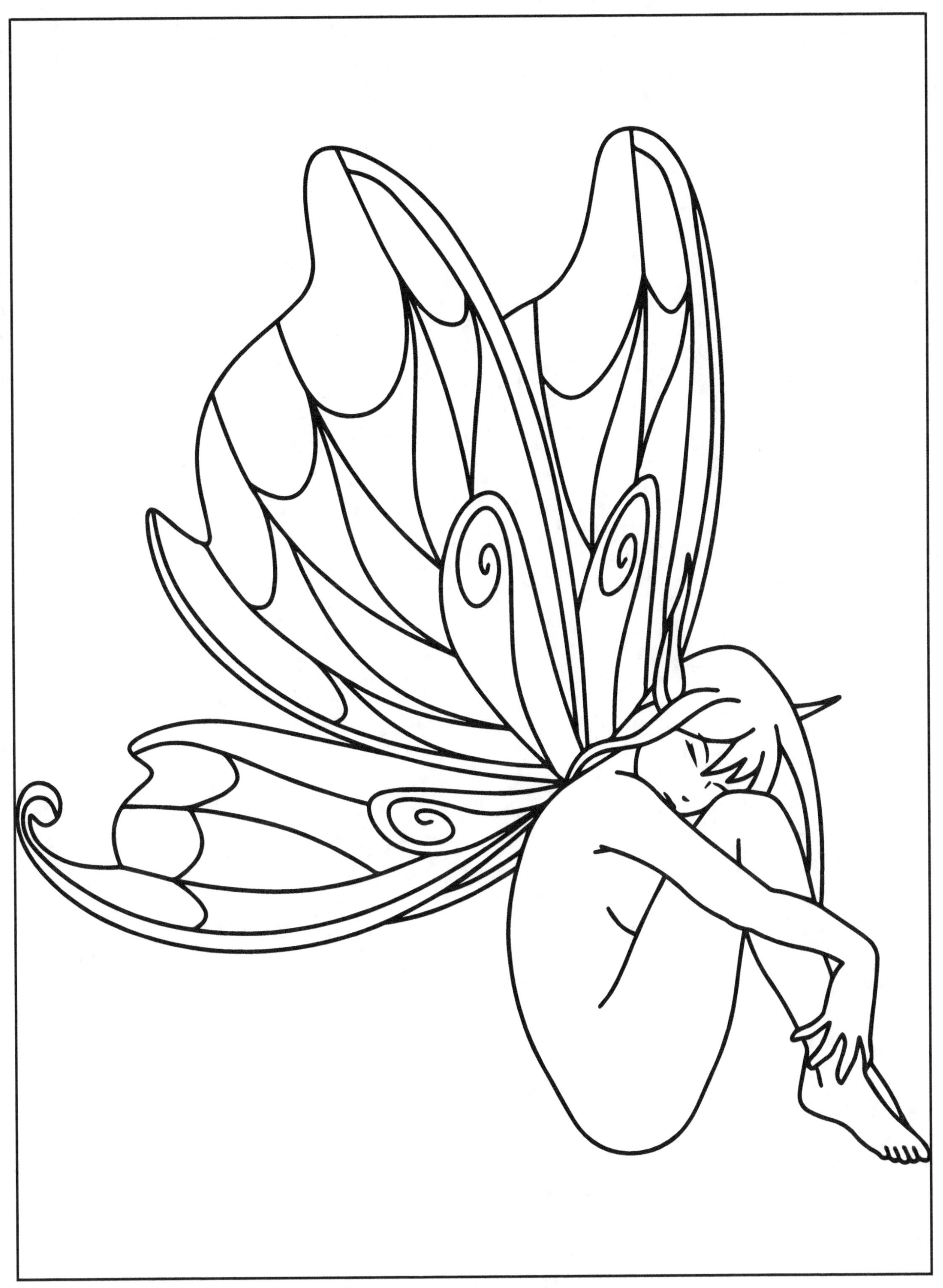

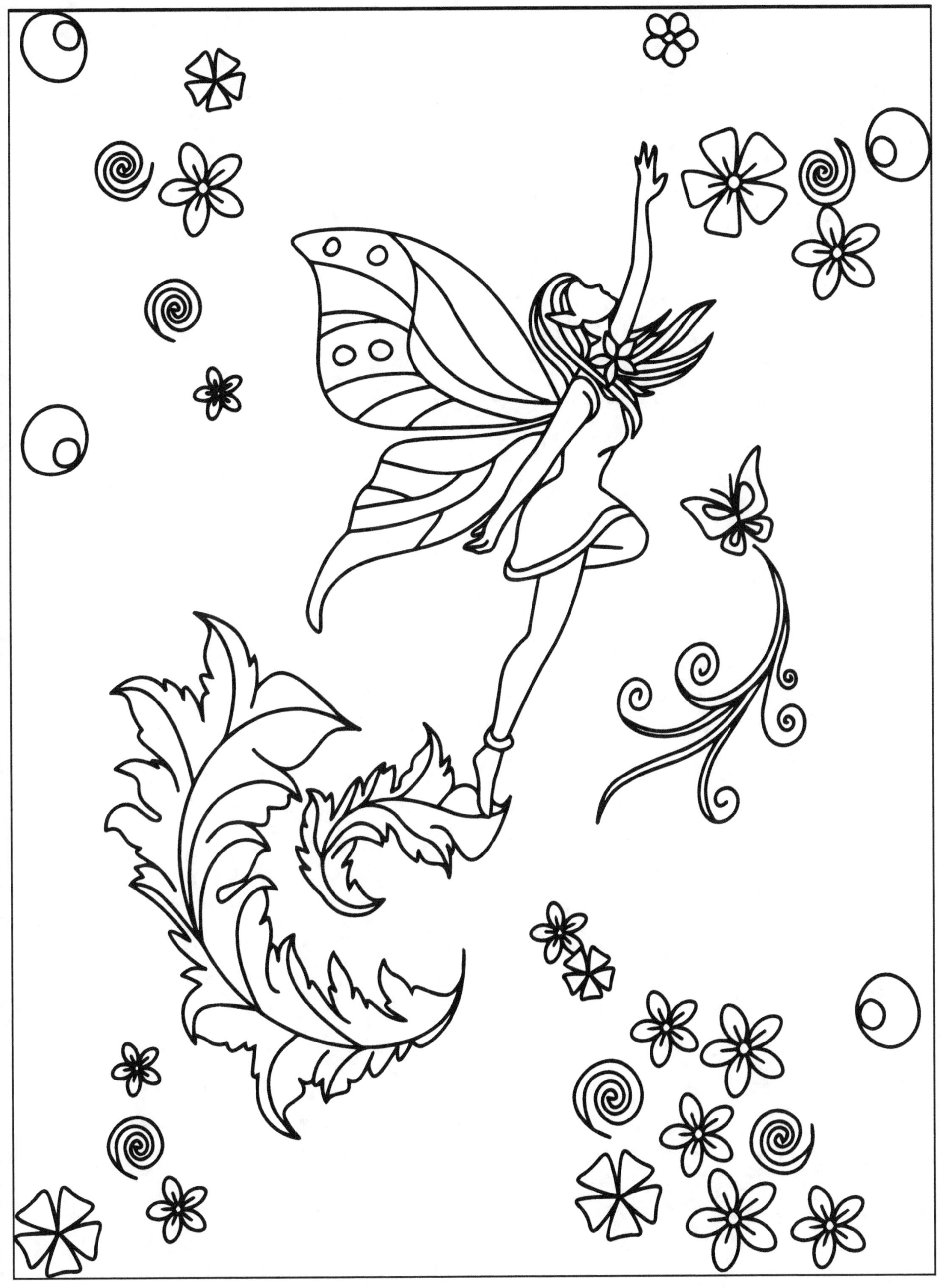

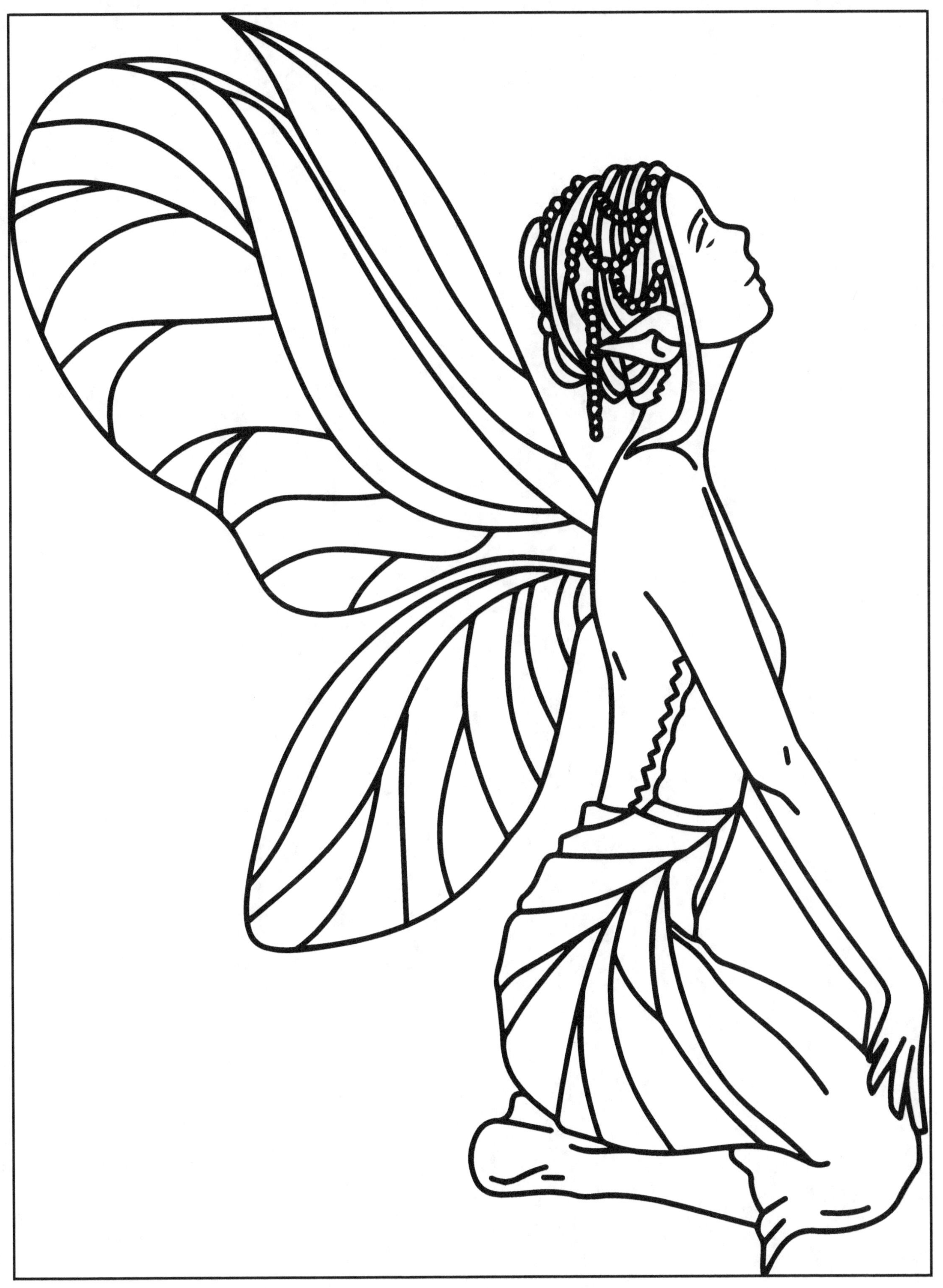

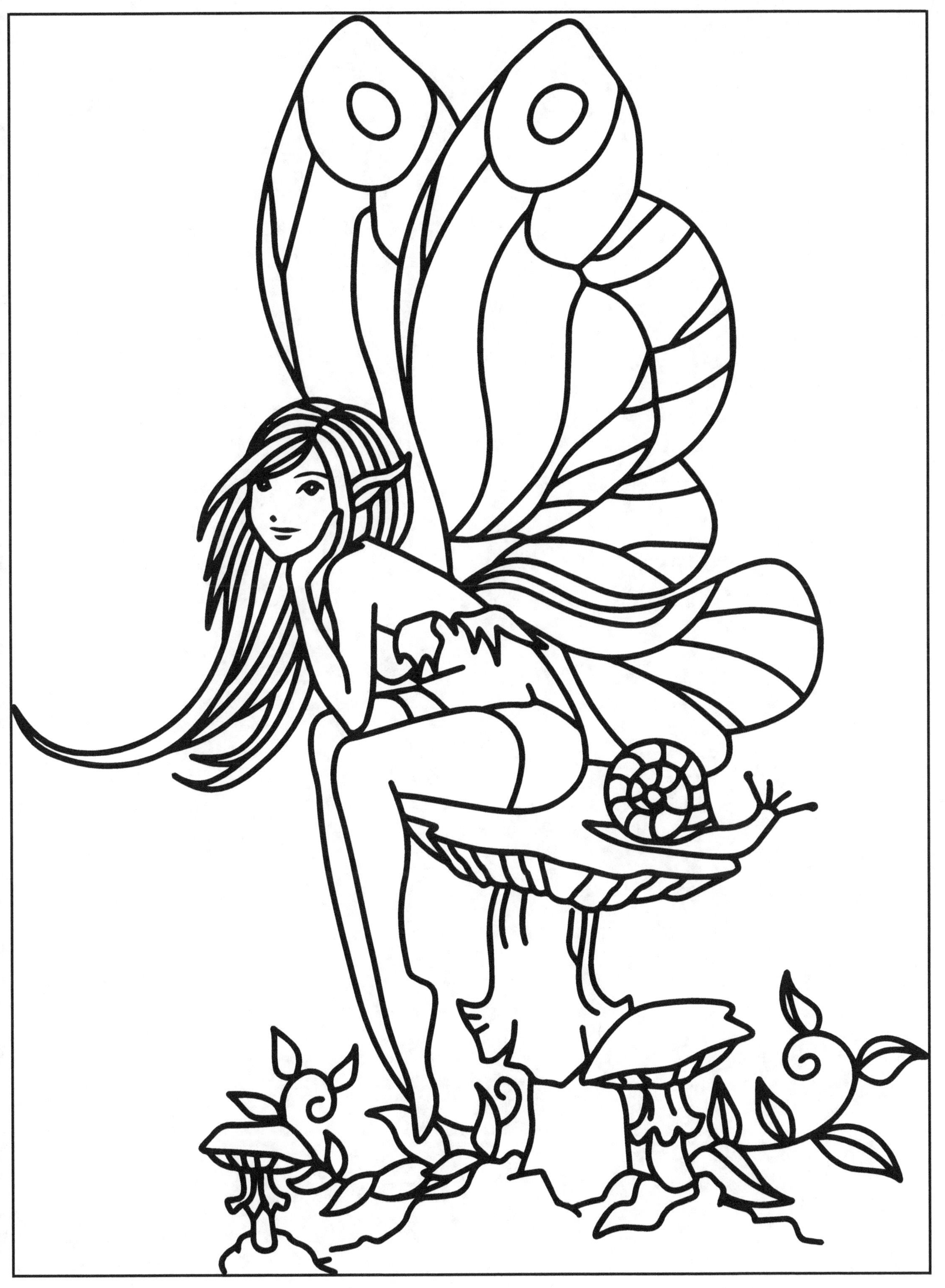

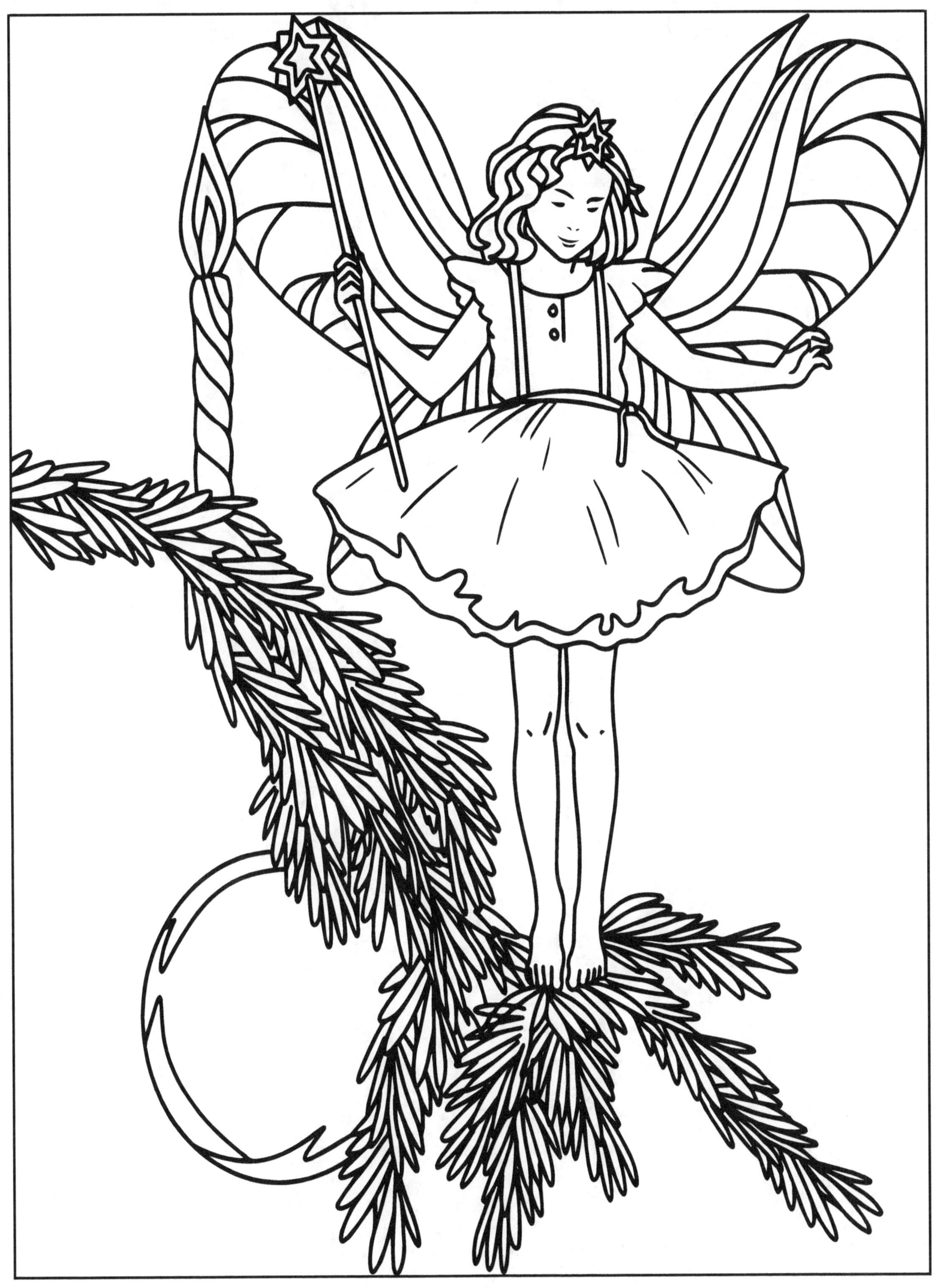

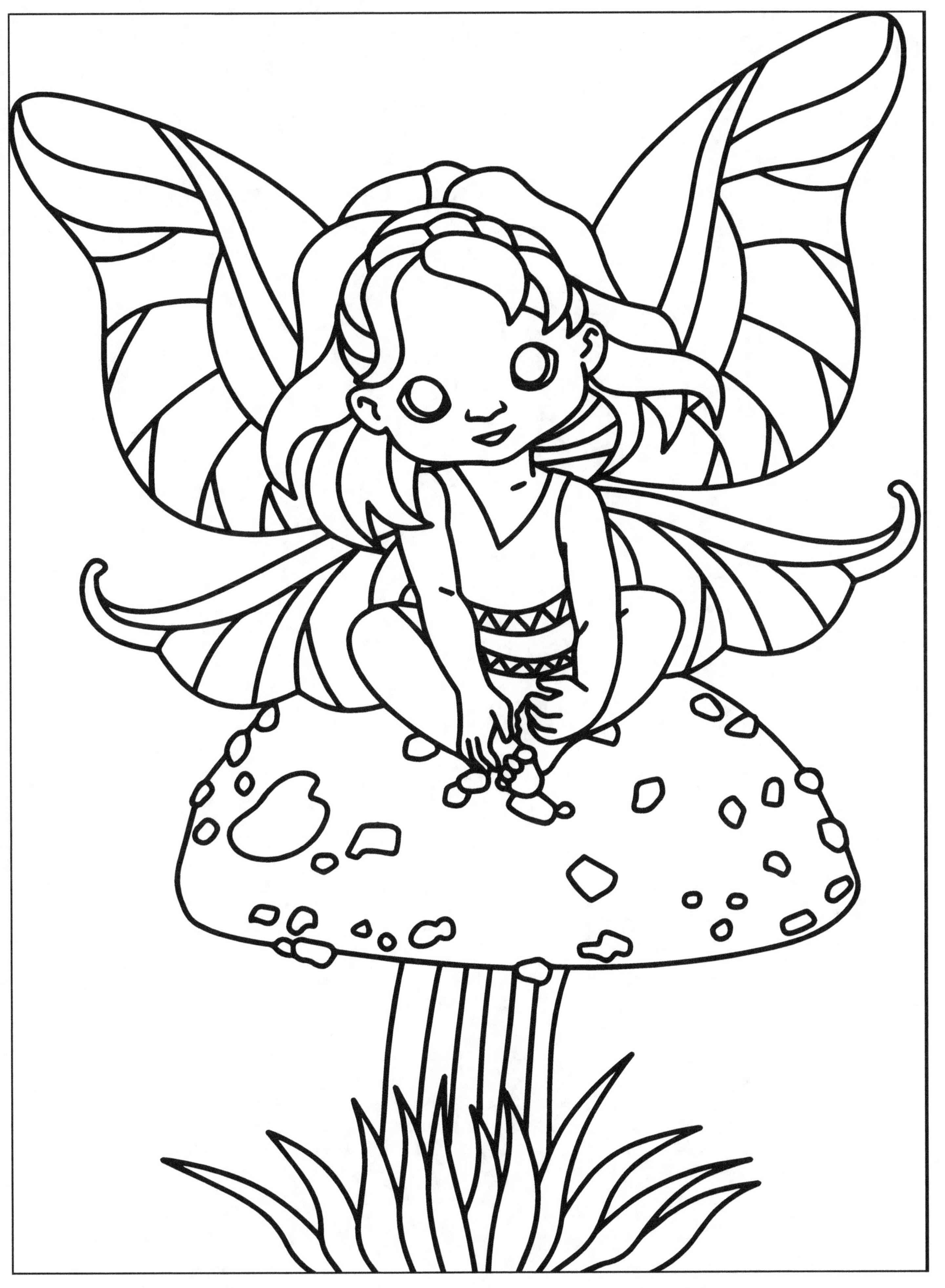

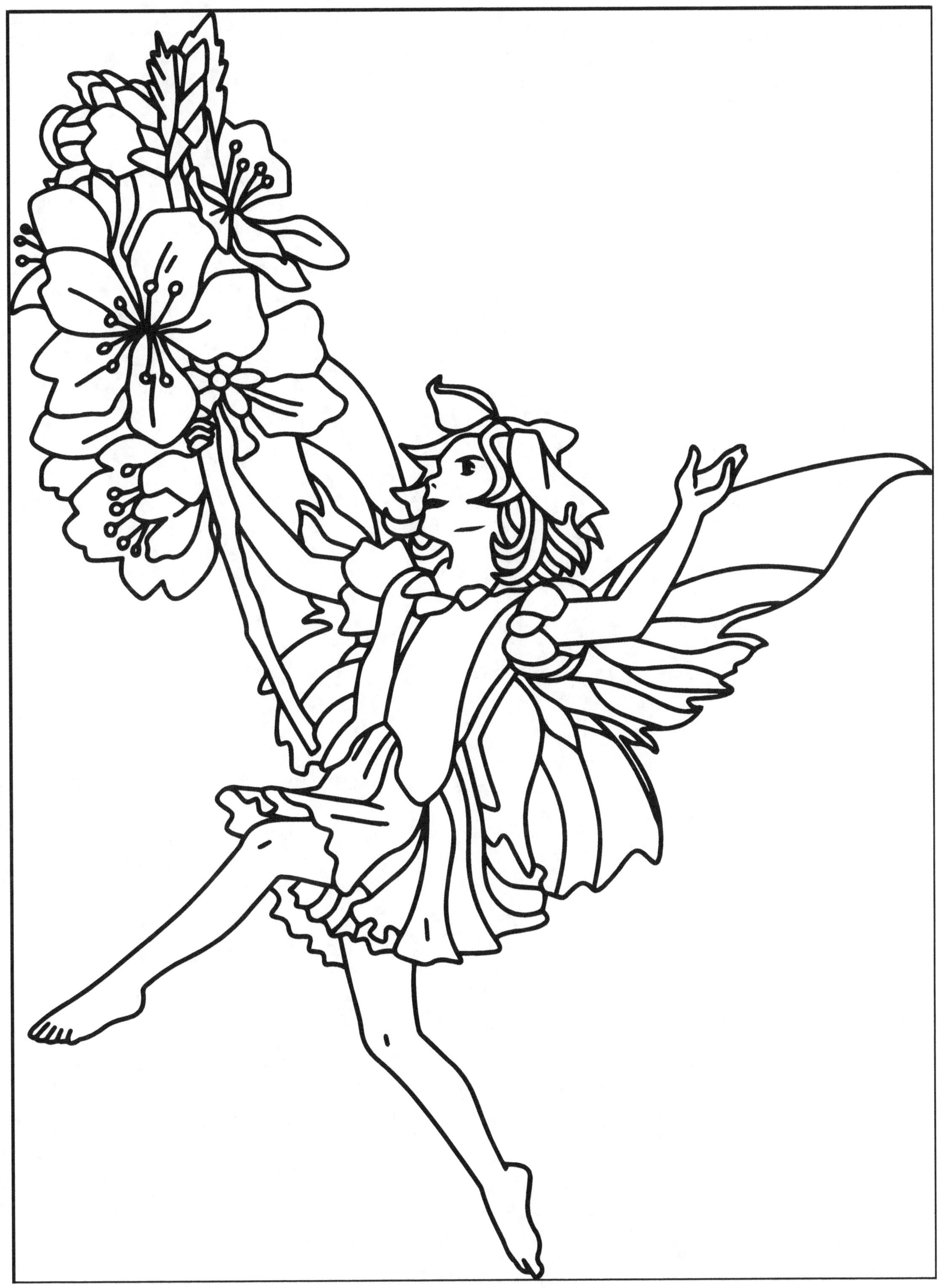

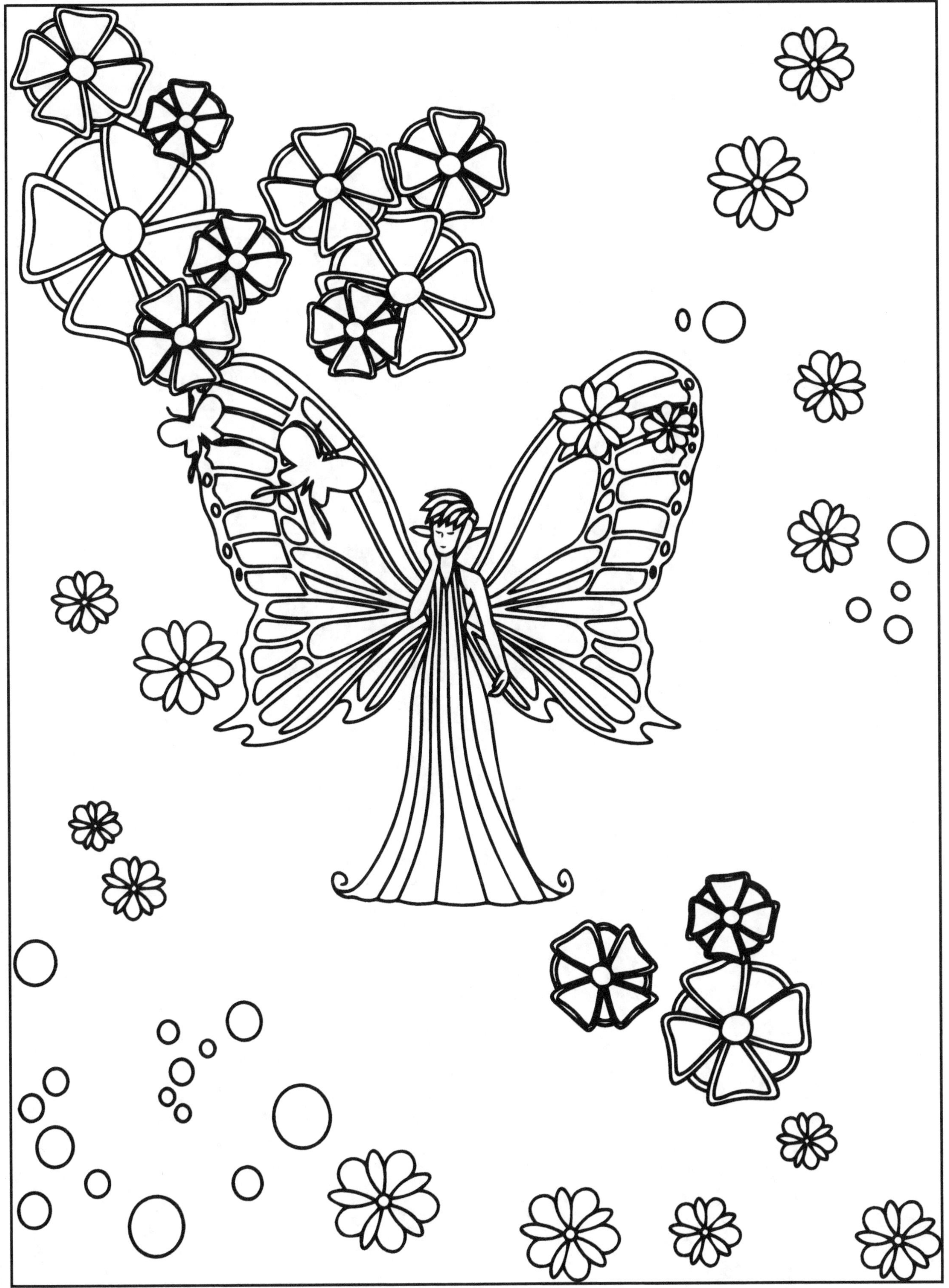

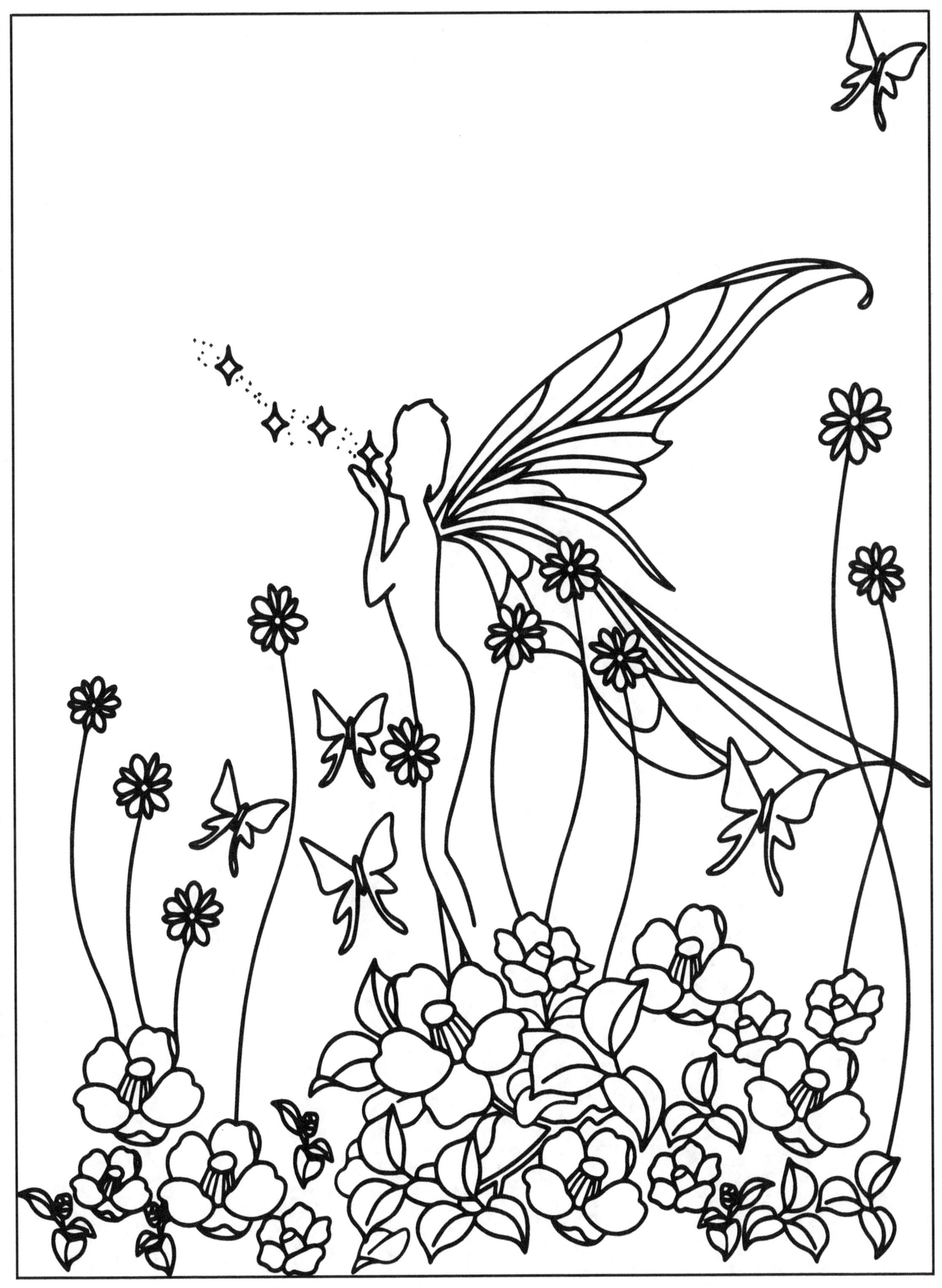

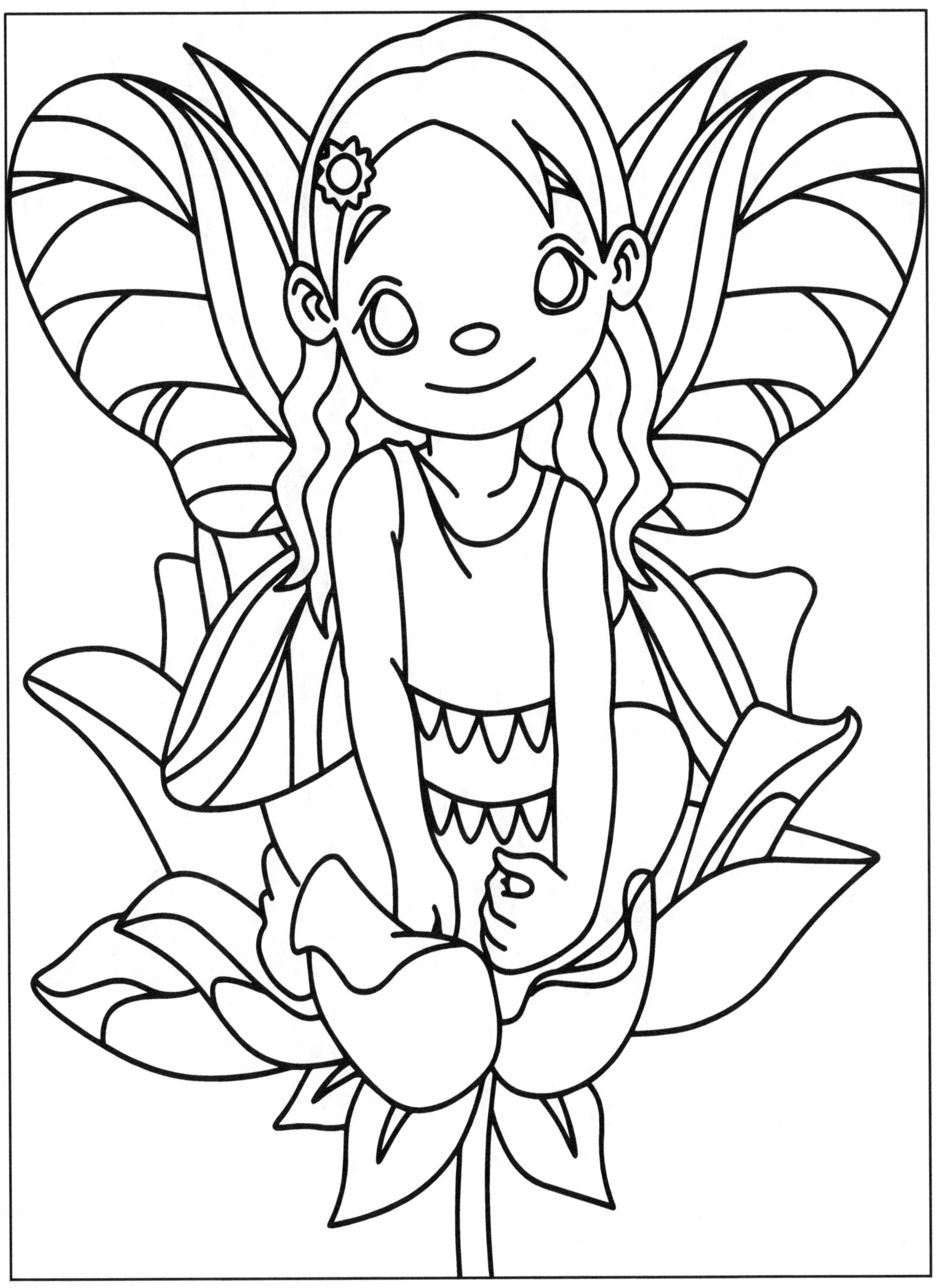

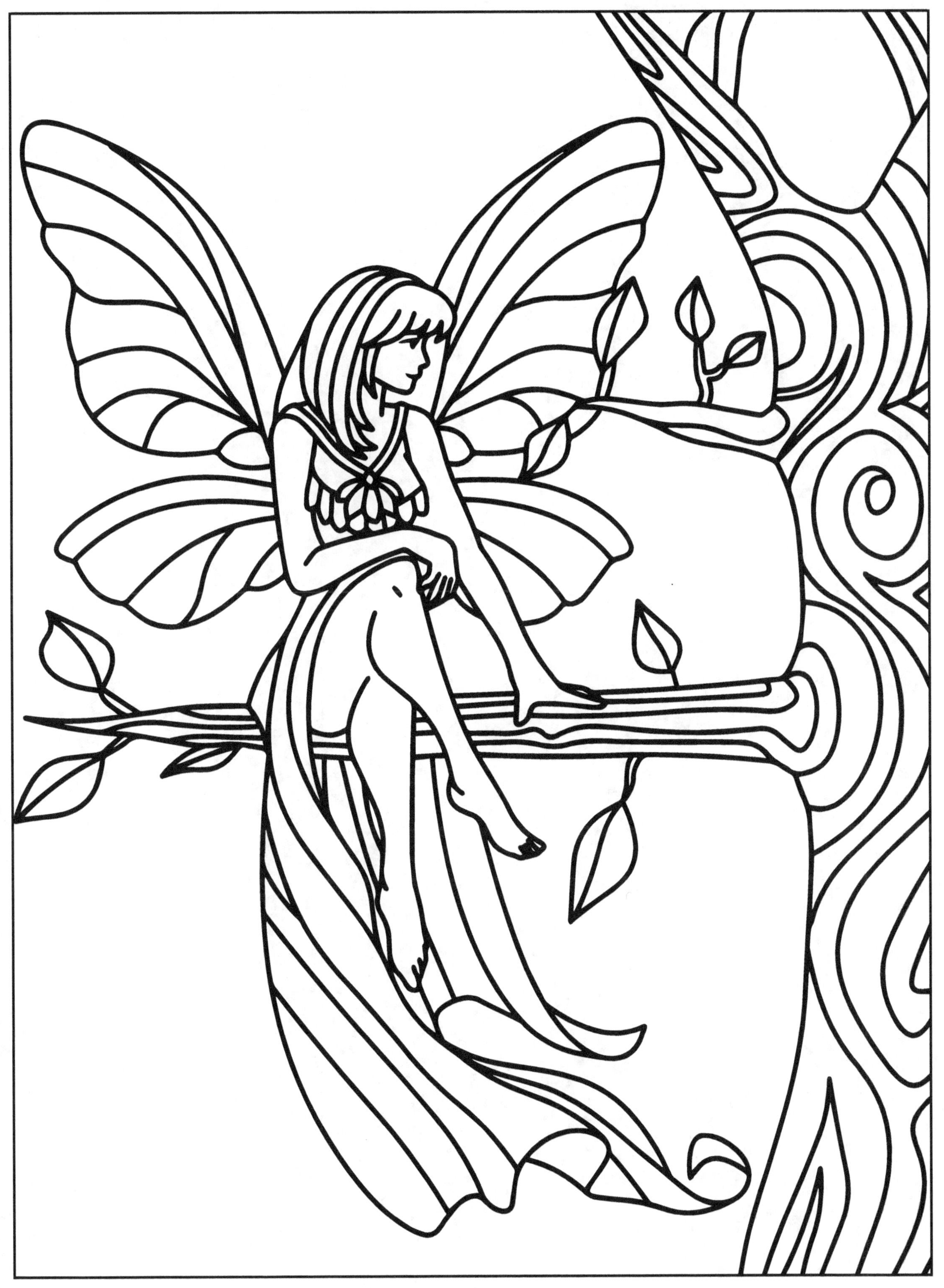

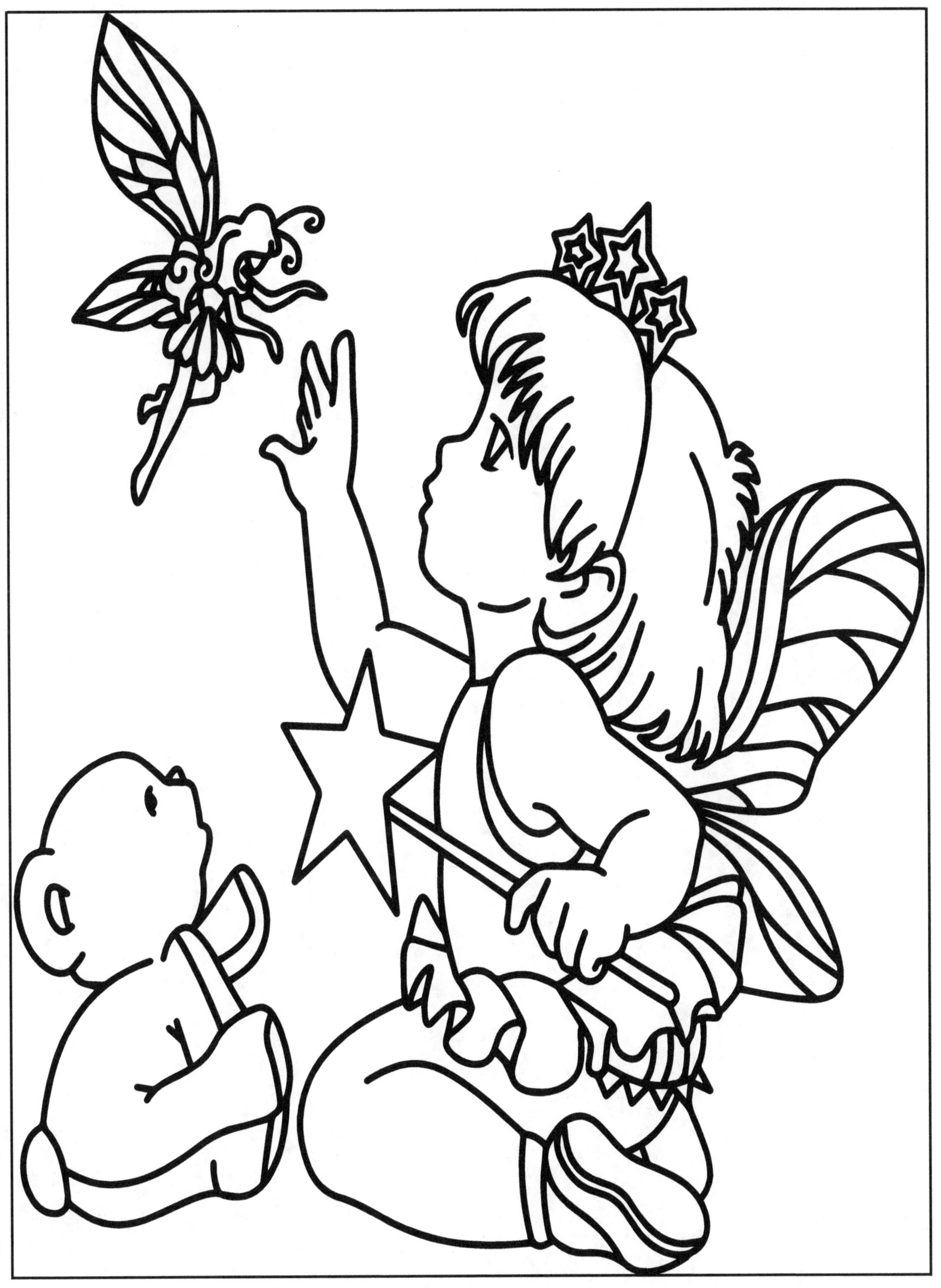

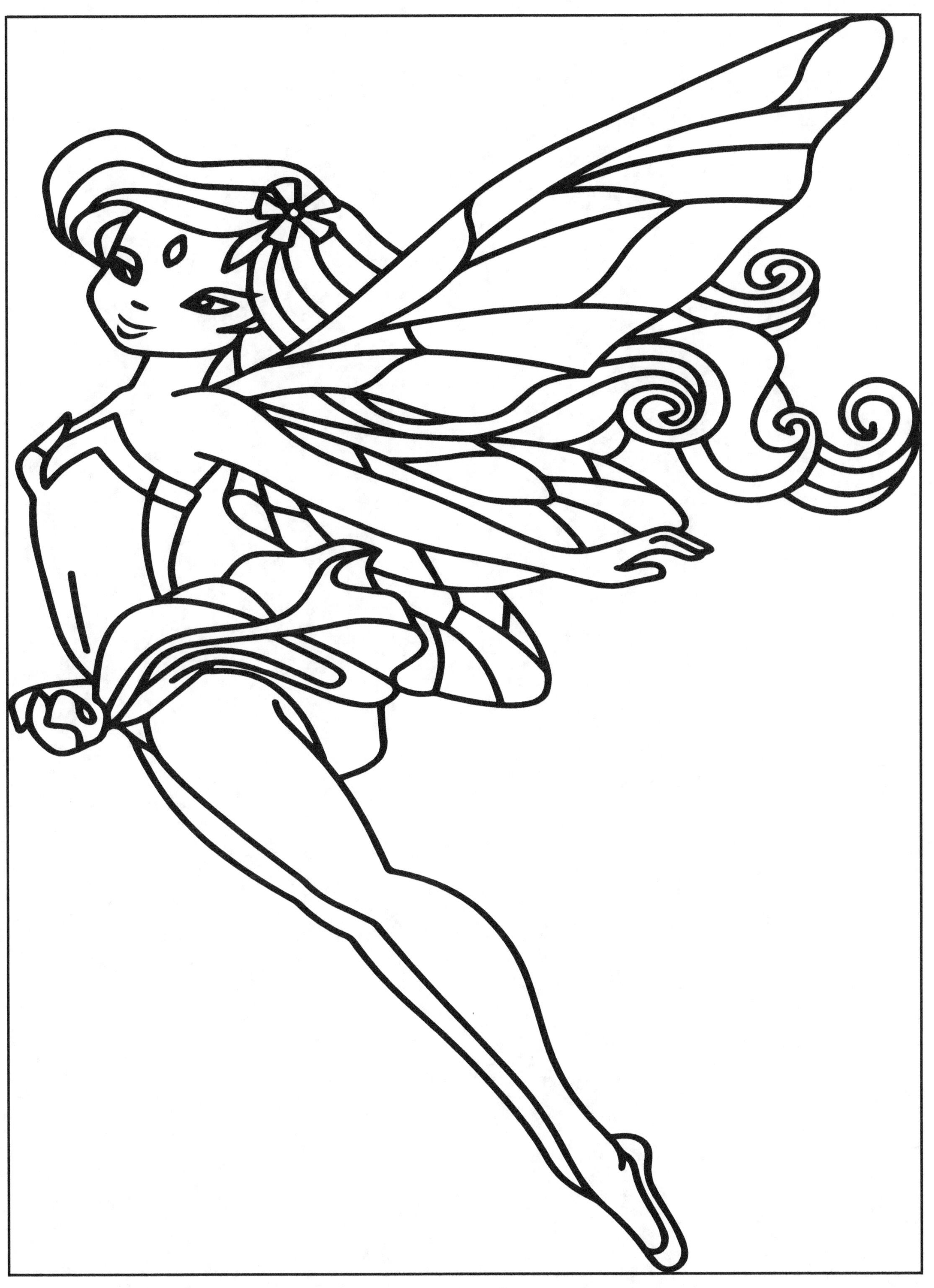

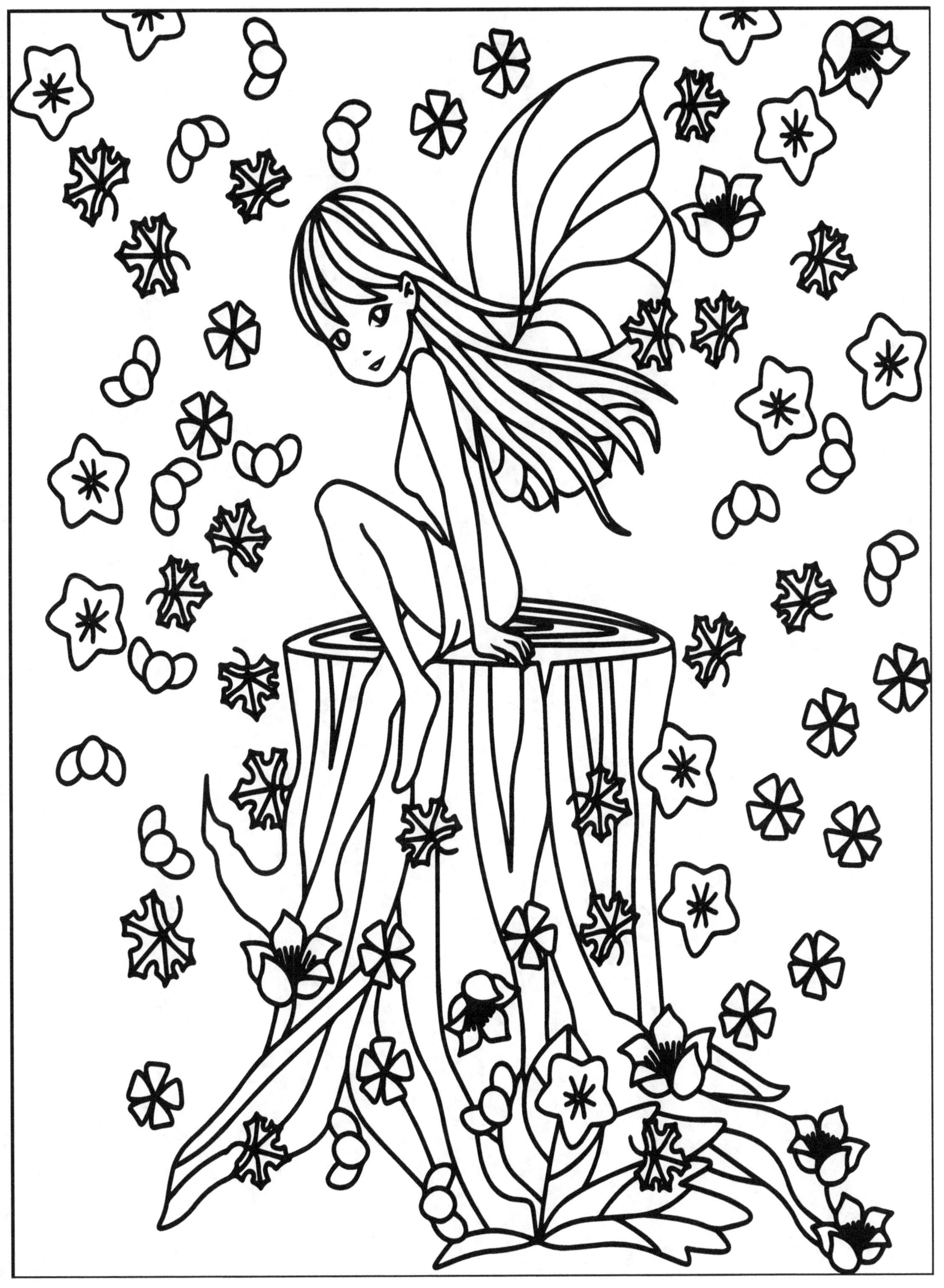

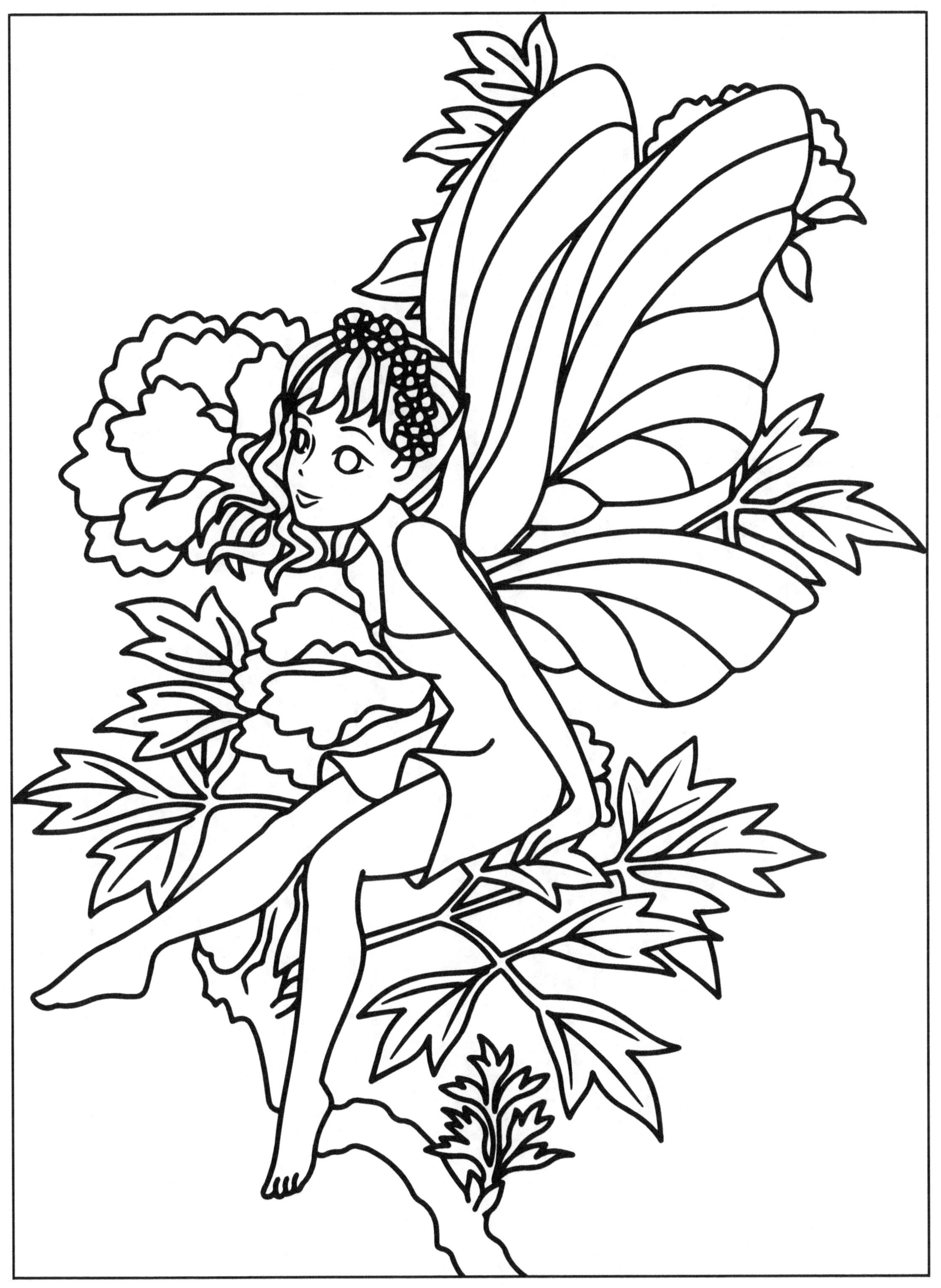

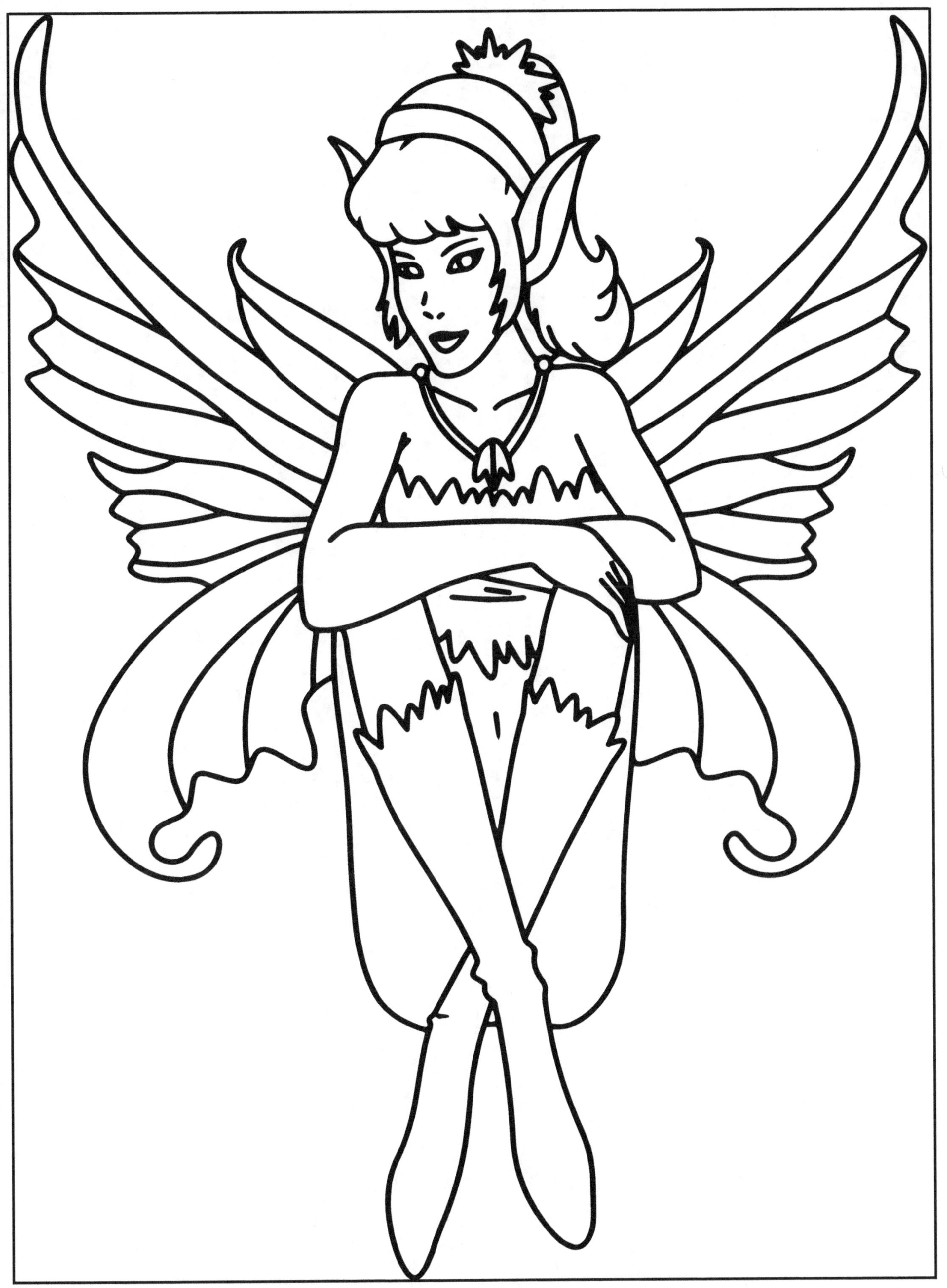

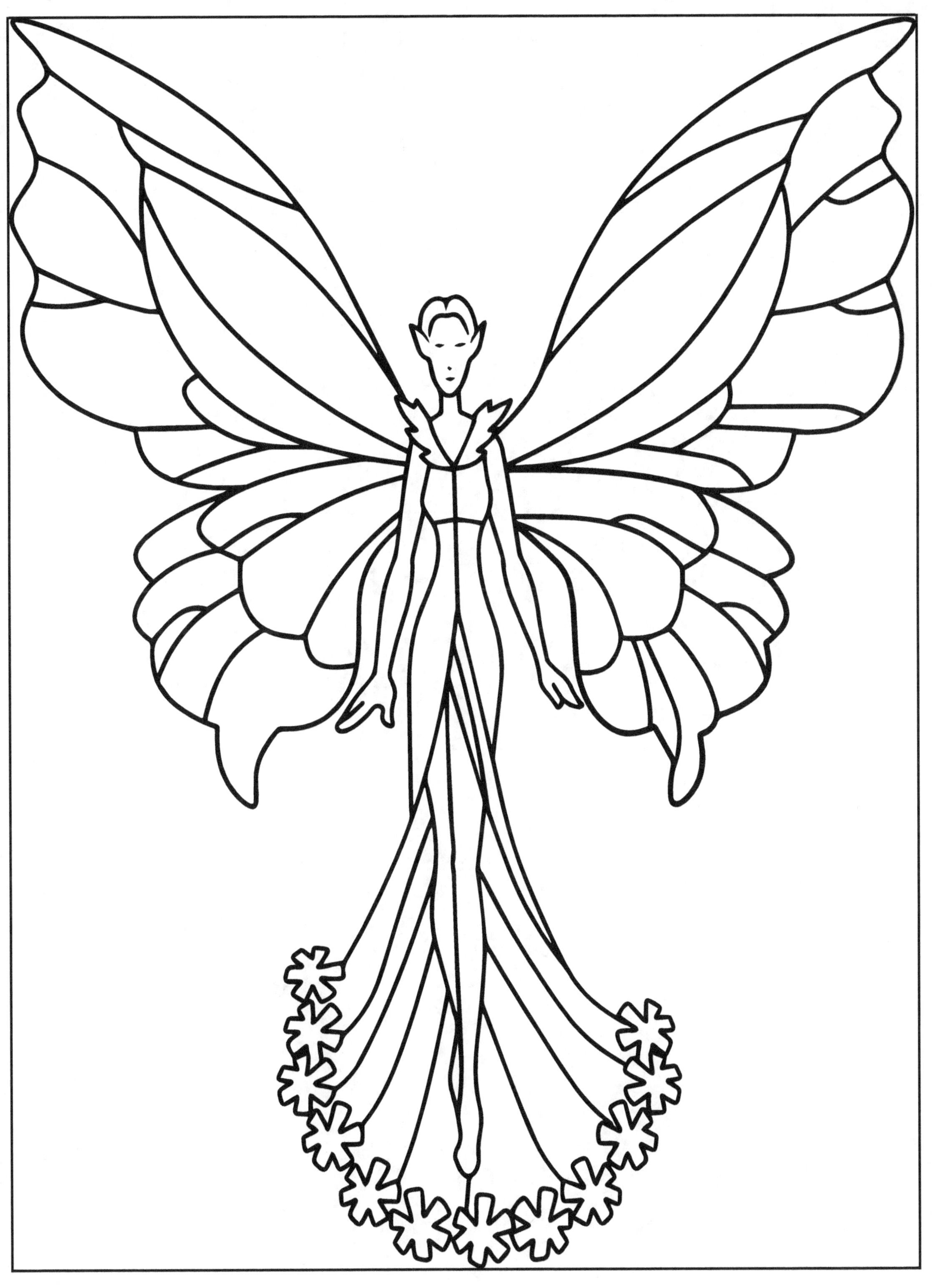

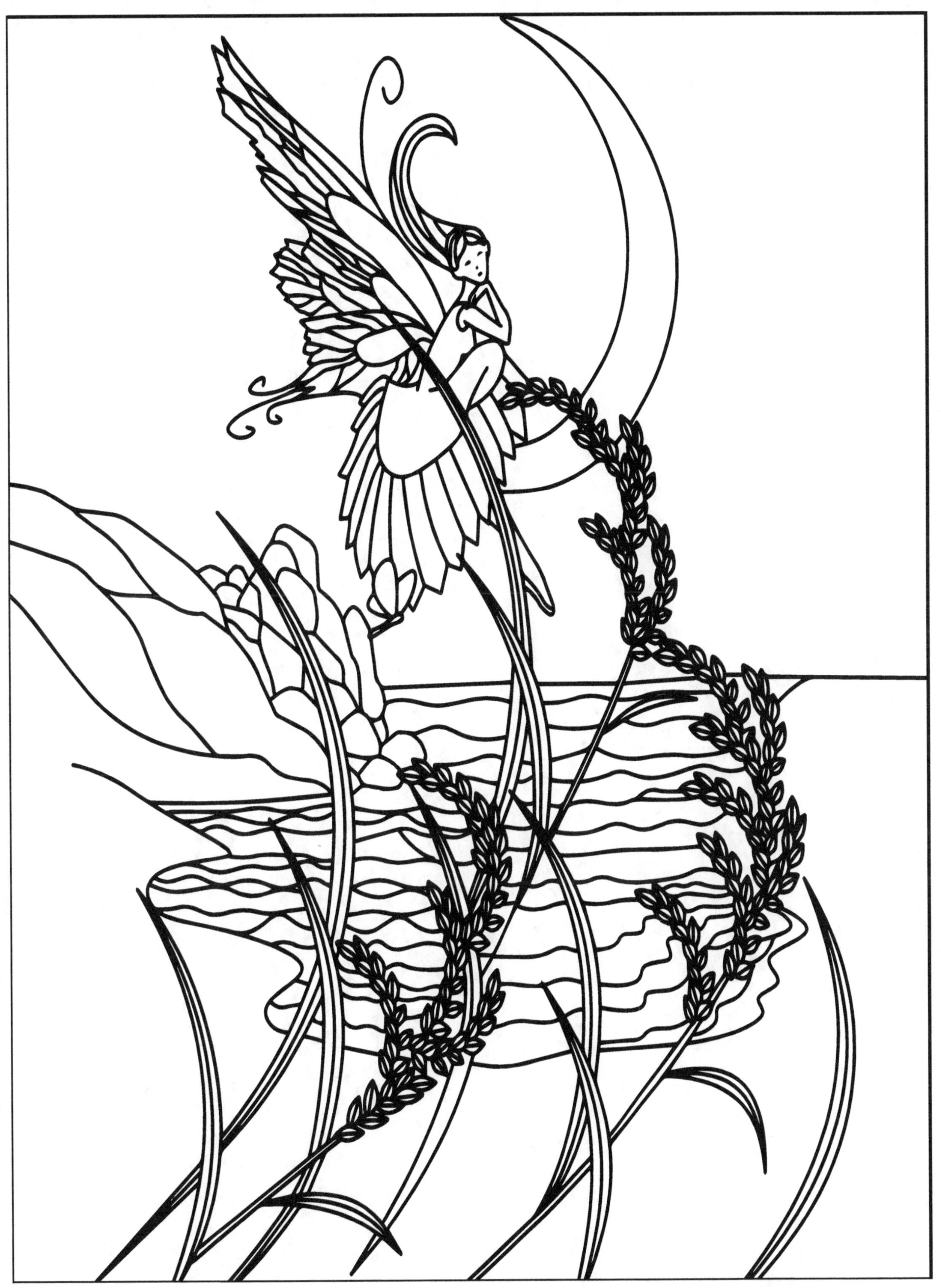

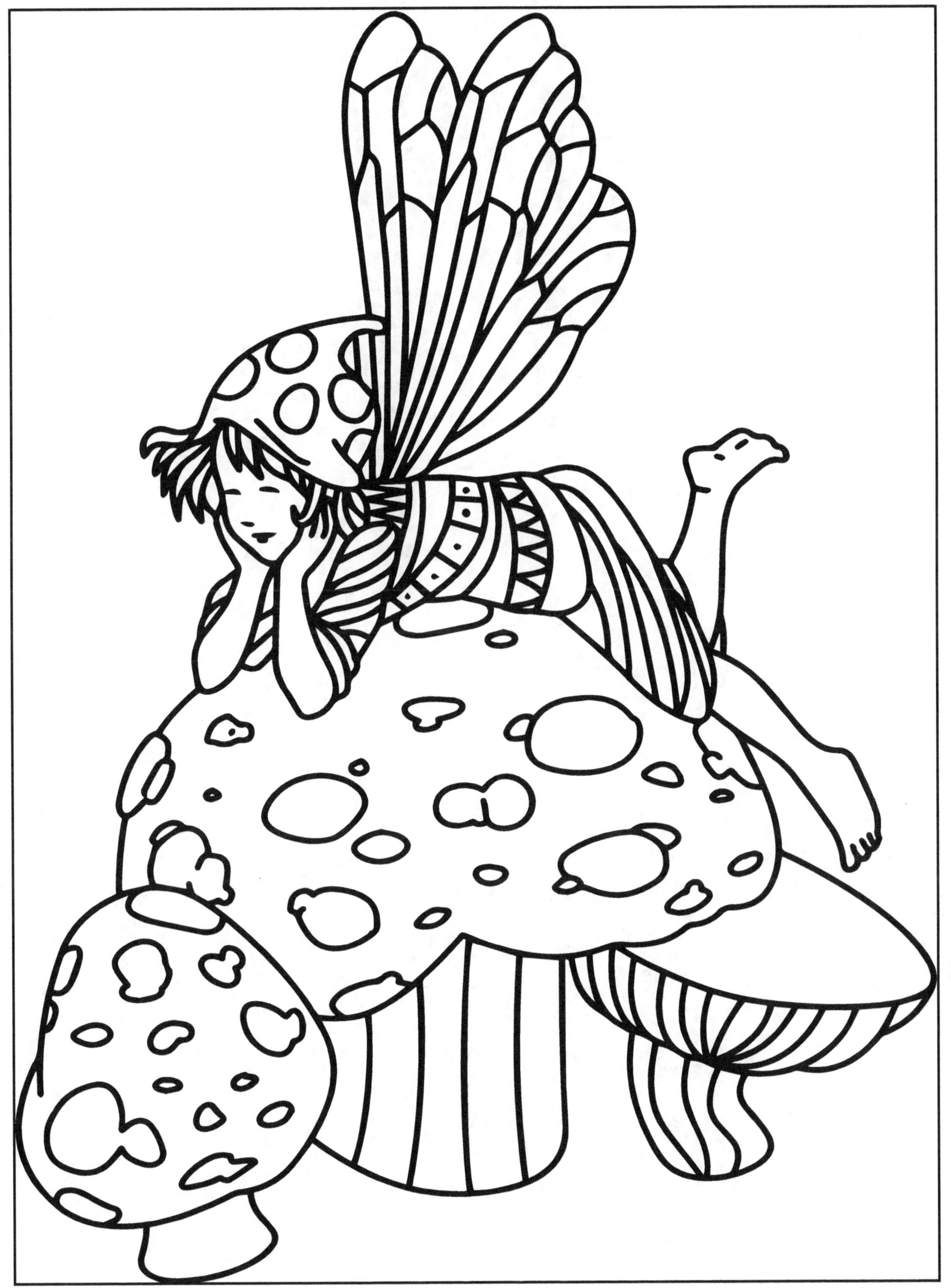

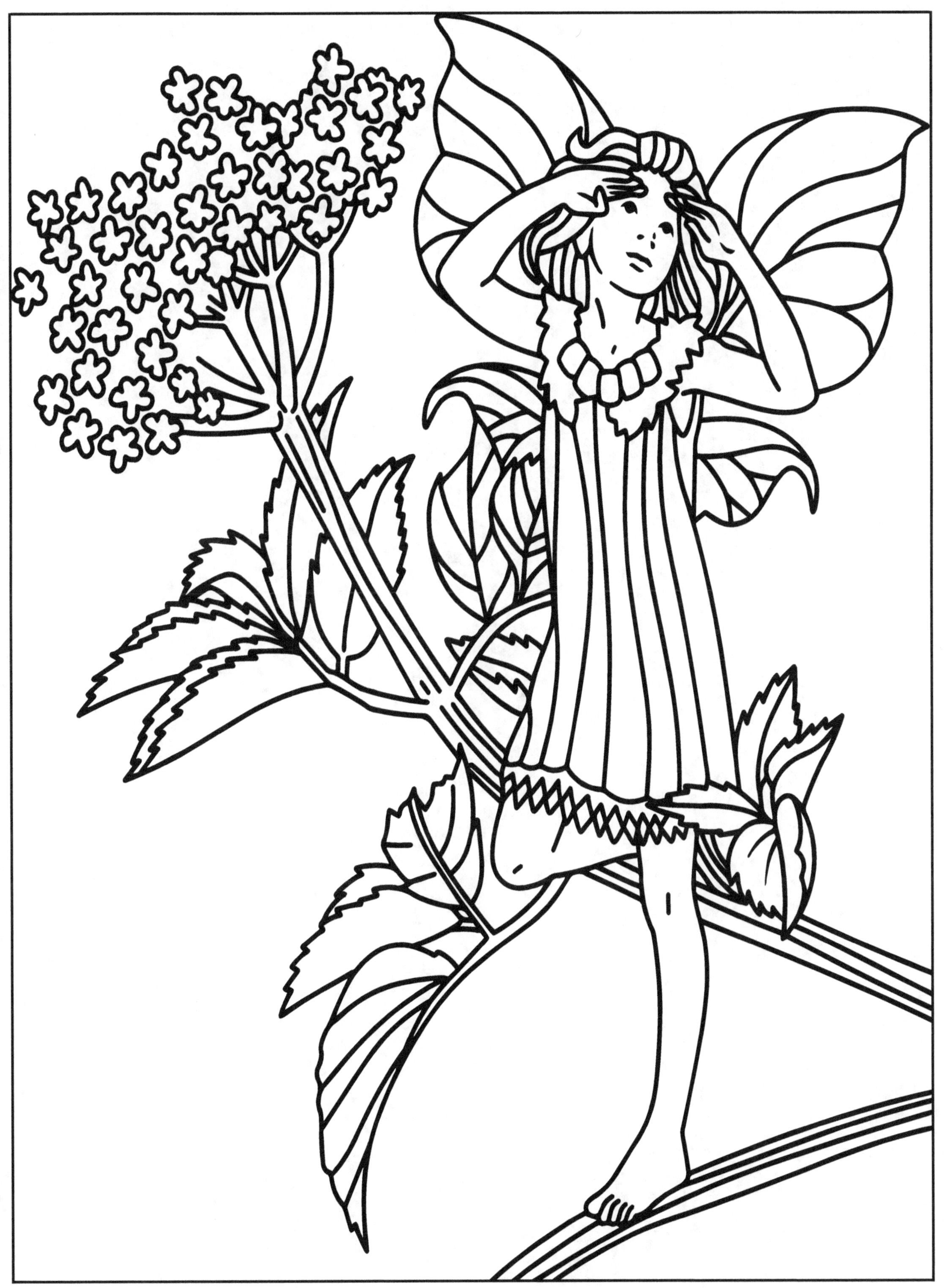

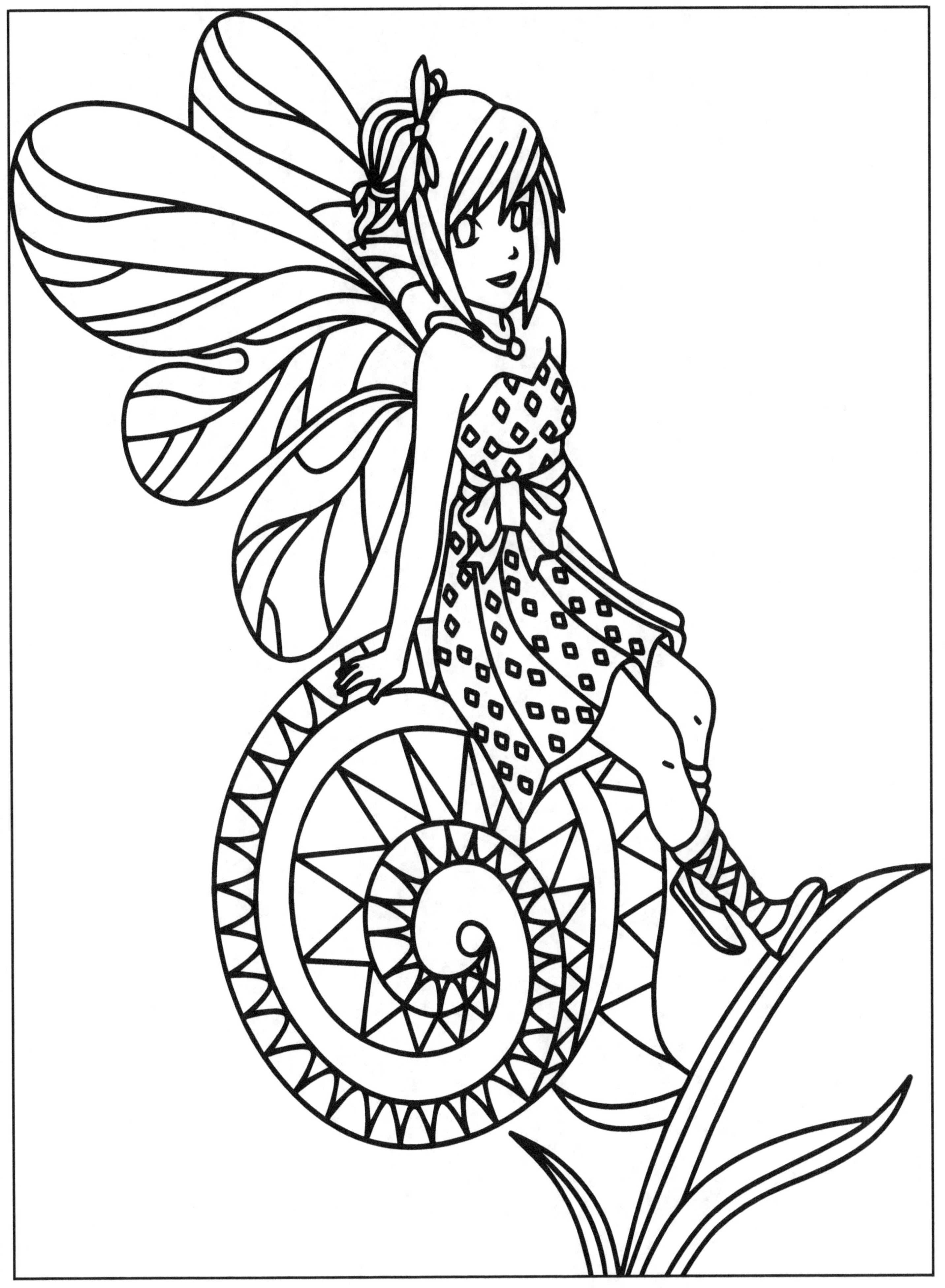

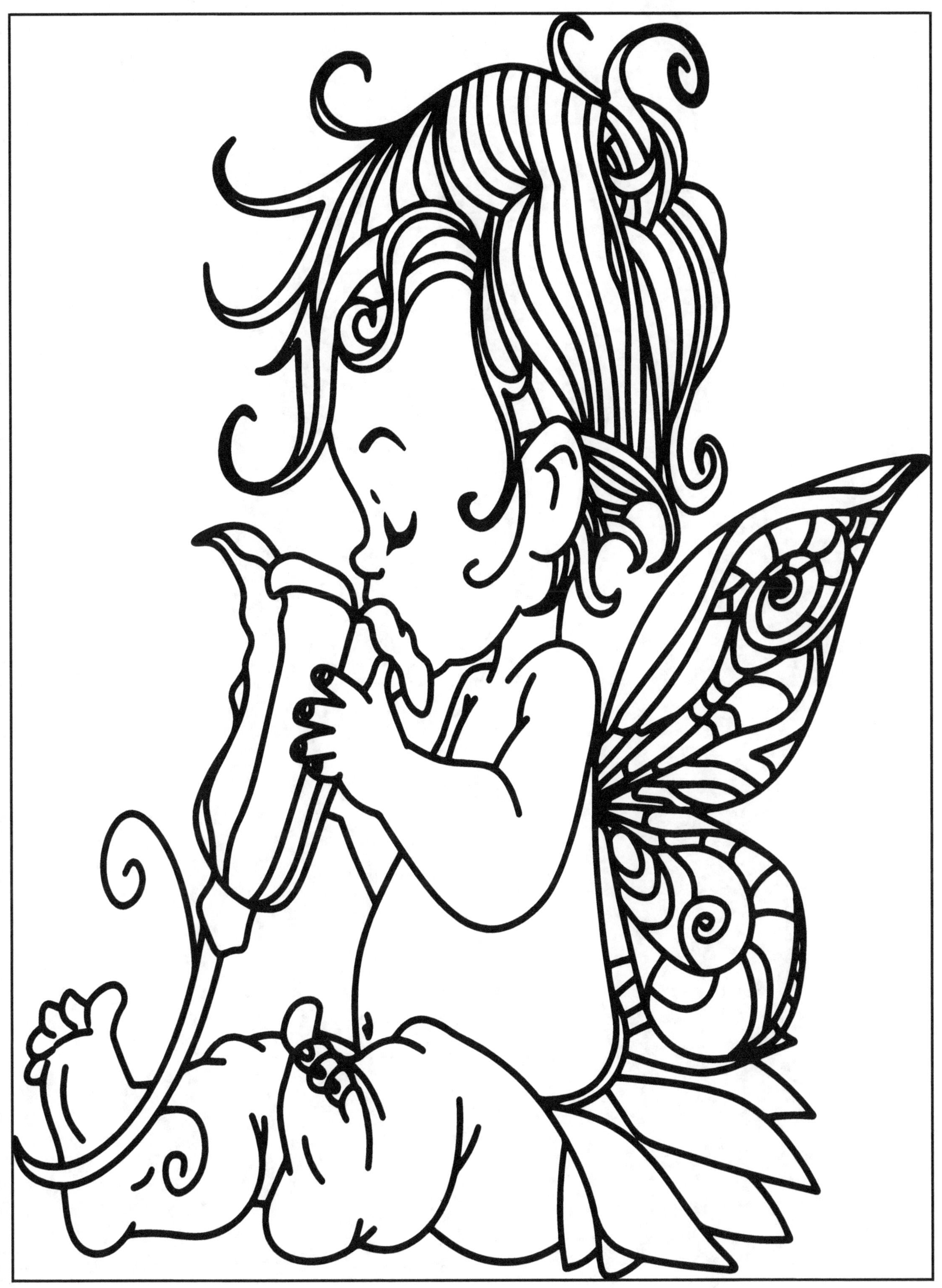

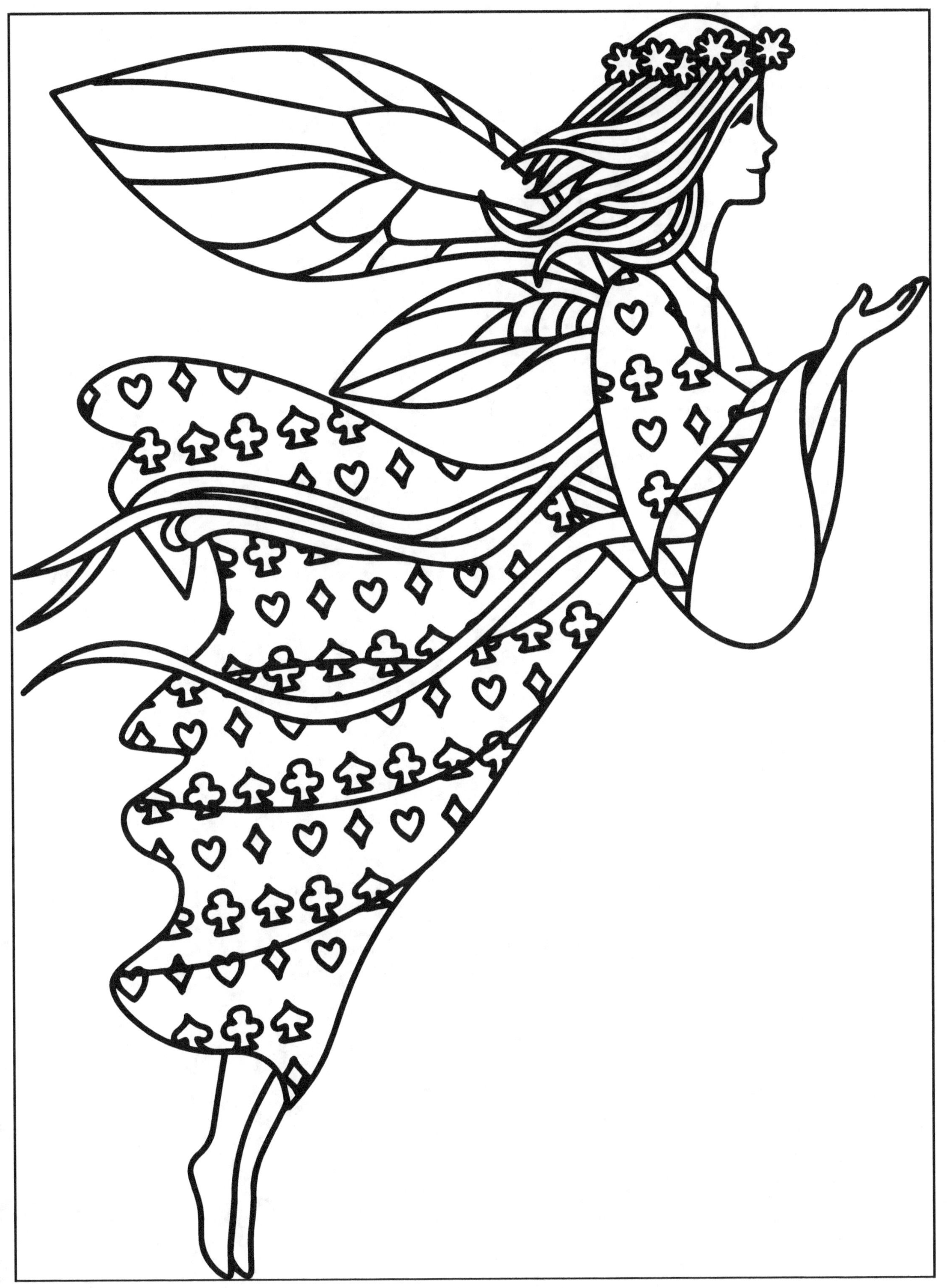

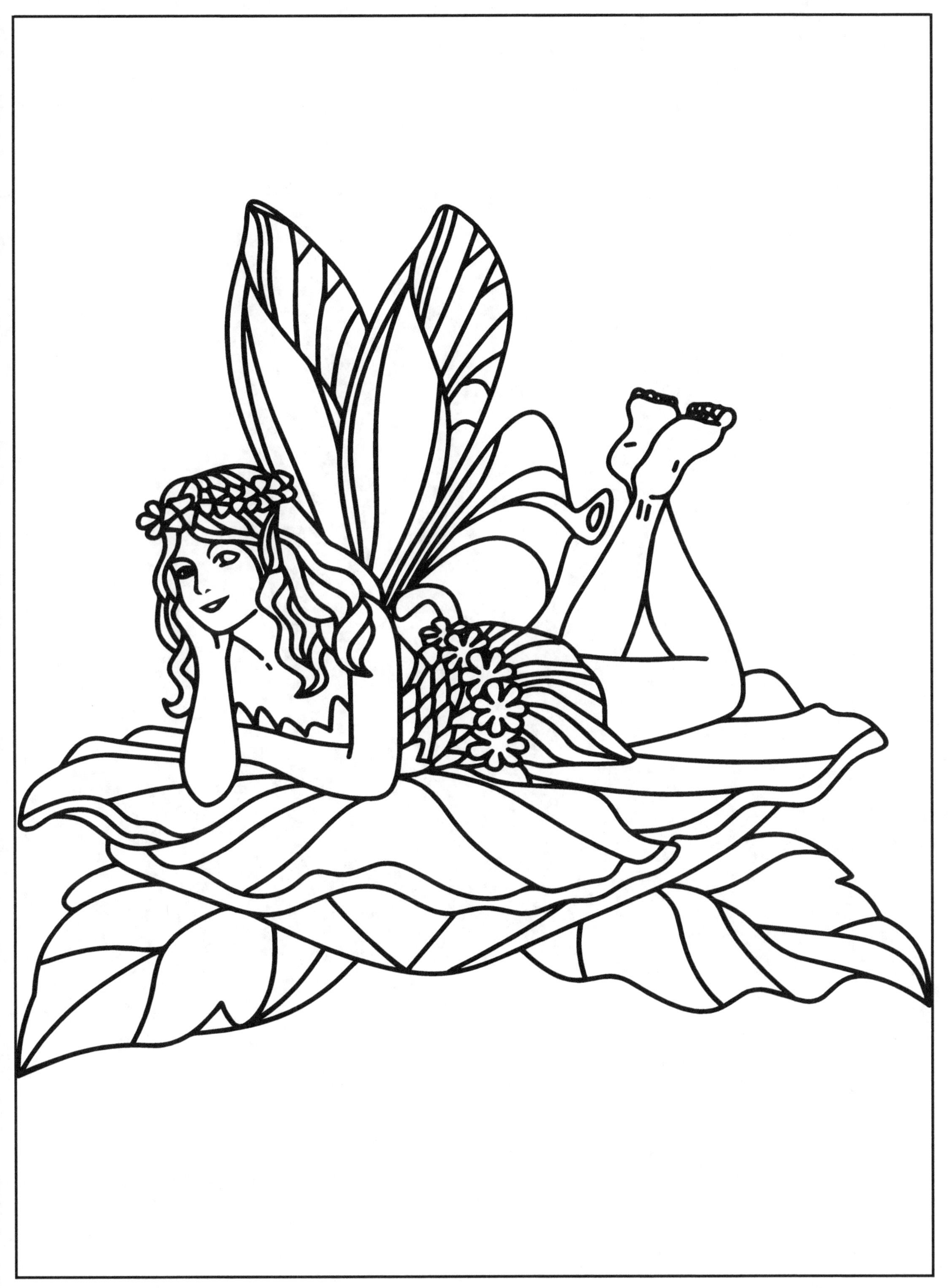

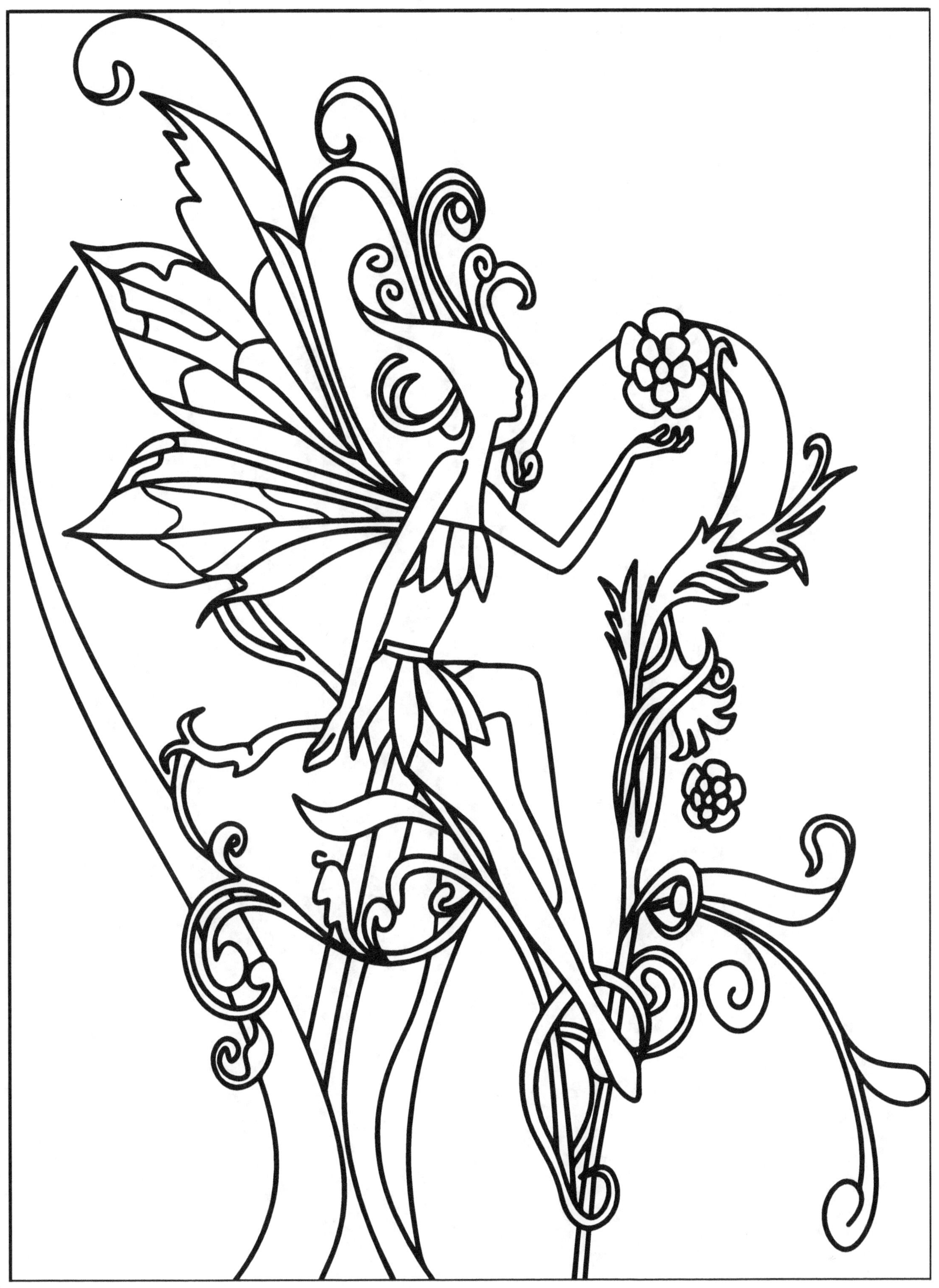

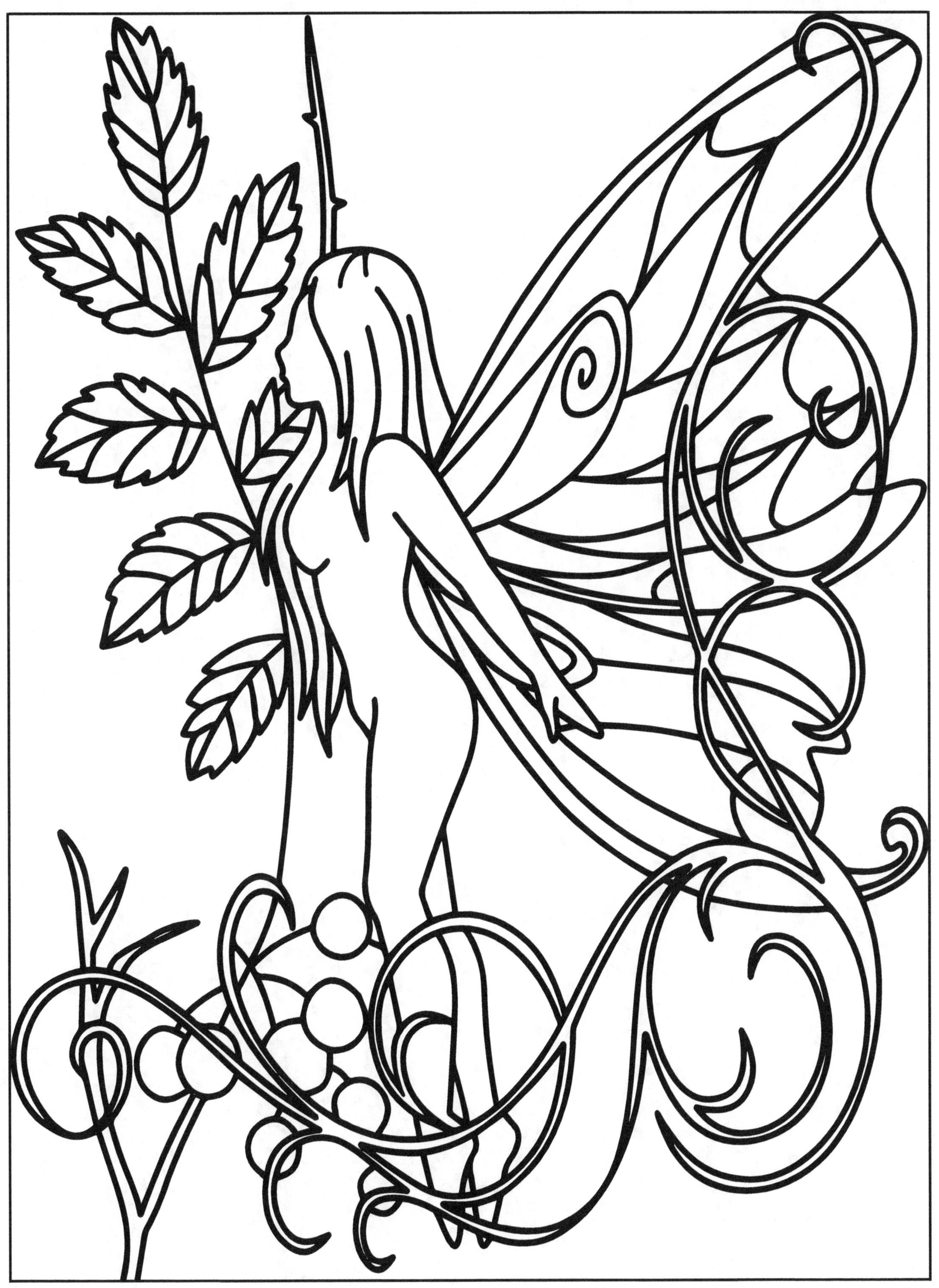

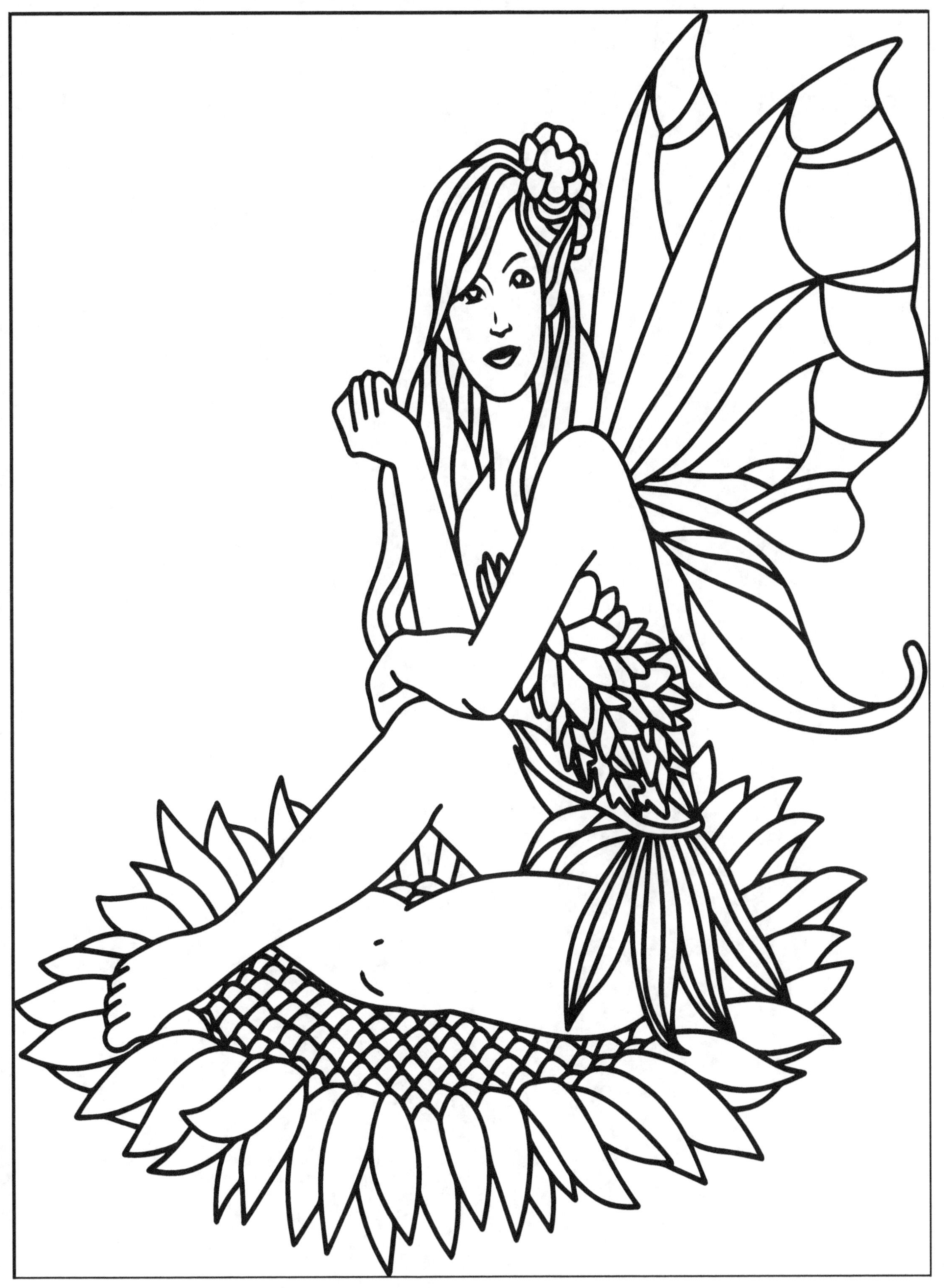

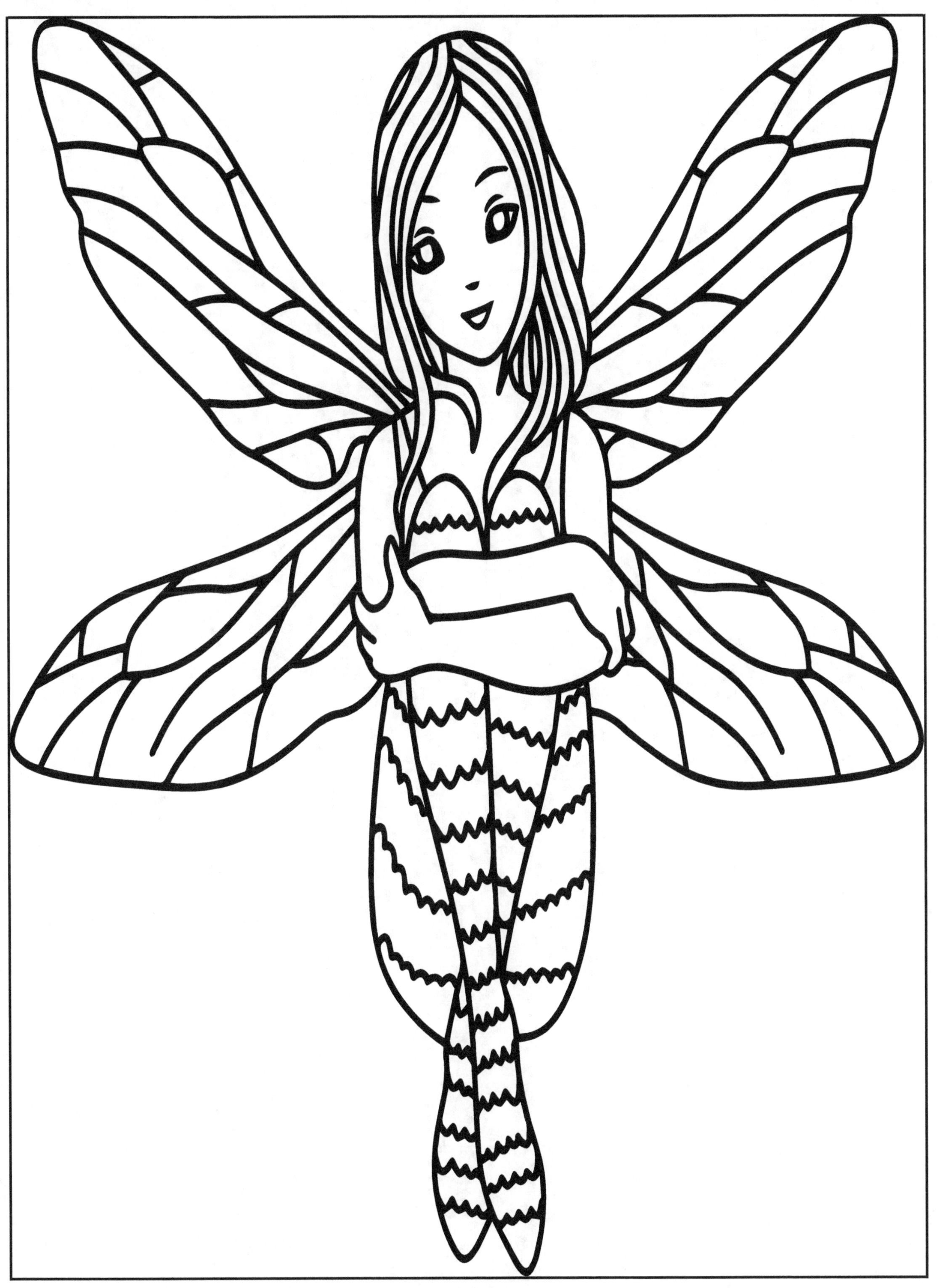

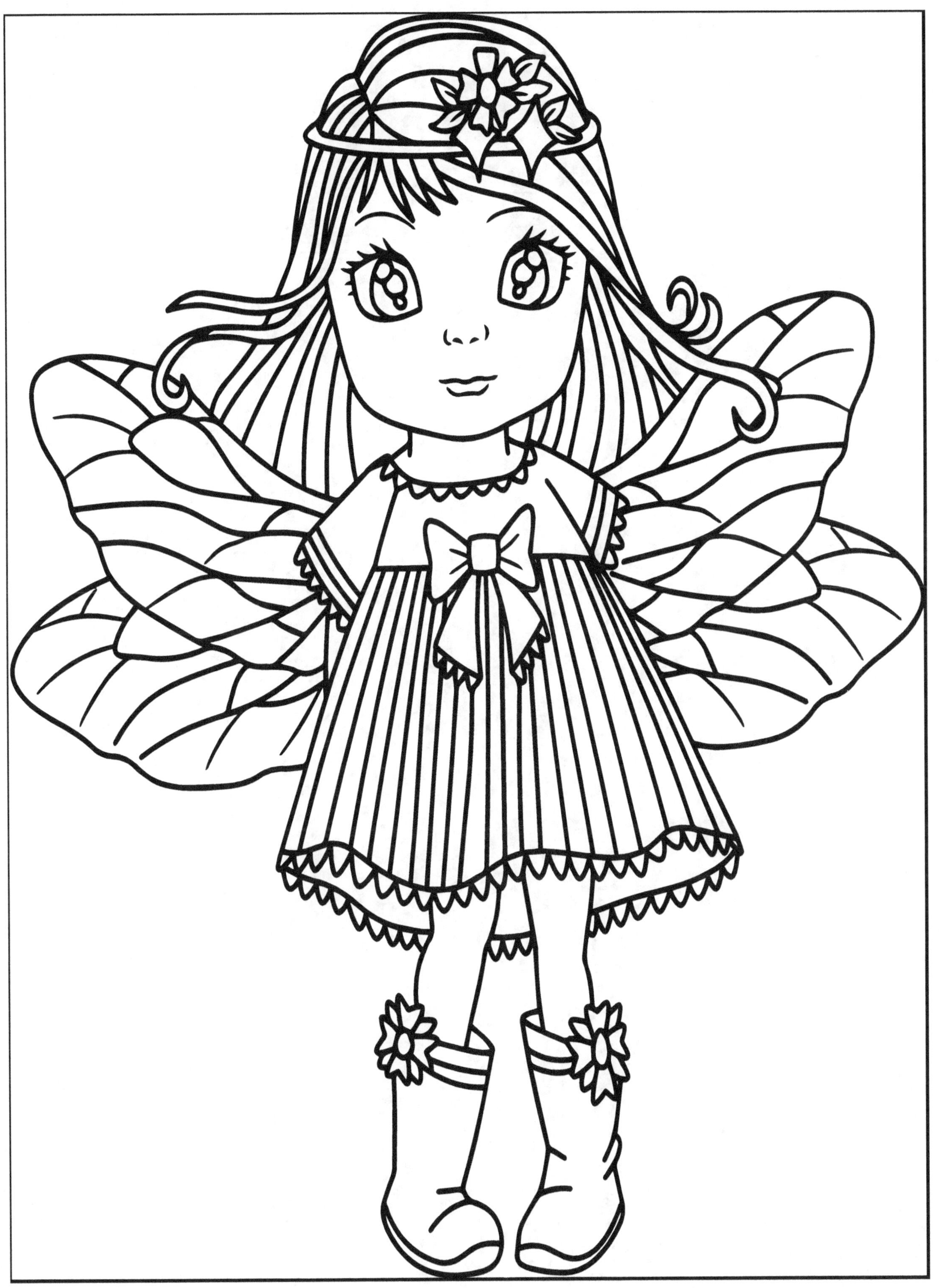

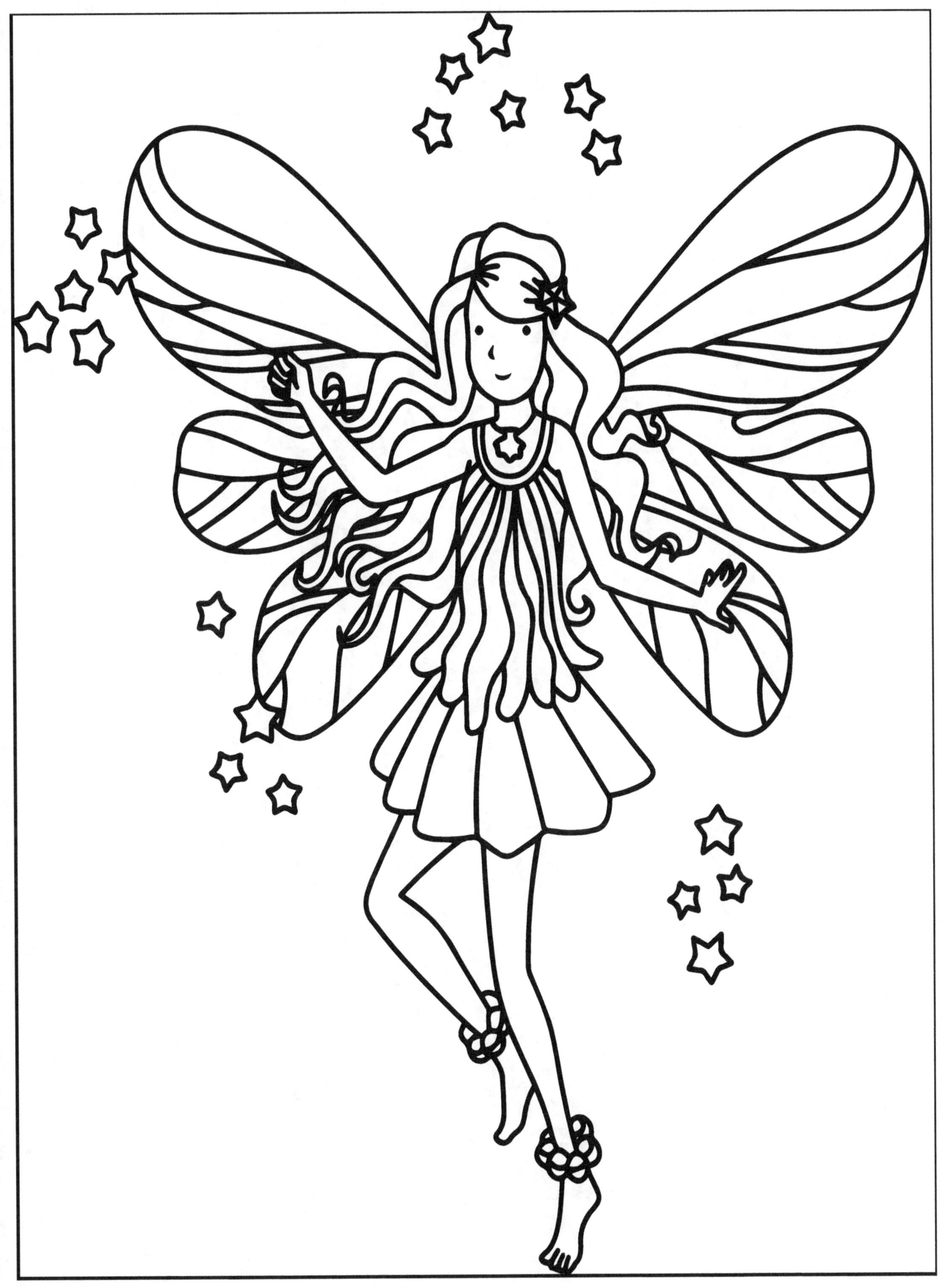